Passages – Transitions – Intersections

Volume 7

General Editors:
Paola Partenza (University of Chieti-Pescara, Italy)
Andrea Mariani (University of Chieti-Pescara, Italy)

Advisory Board:
Gianfranca Balestra (University of Siena, Italy)
Barbara M. Benedict (Trinity College Connecticut, USA)
Gert Buelens (University of Ghent, Belgium)
Jennifer Kilgore-Caradec (University of Caen, and ICP, France)
Esra Melikoglu (University of Istanbul, Turkey)
Michal Peprník (University of Olomouc, Czech Republic)
John Paul Russo (University of Miami, USA)

Michele Russo

A Plurilingual Analysis of Four Russian-American Autobiographies

Cournos, Nabokov, Berberova, Shteyngart

V&R unipress

Bibliographic information published by the Deutsche Nationalbibliothek
The Deutsche Nationalbibliothek lists this publication in the Deutsche Nationalbibliografie;
detailed bibliographic data are available online: https://dnb.de.

This volume is published with the contribution of the Department of Modern Languages,
Literatures and Cultures, University "G. d'Annunzio", Chieti-Pescara.

© 2020, Vandenhoeck & Ruprecht GmbH & Co. KG, Theaterstraße 13, 37073 Göttingen, Germany
All rights reserved. No part of this work may be reproduced or utilized in any form or by any means,
electronic or mechanical, including photocopying, recording, or any information storage and
retrieval system, without prior written permission from the publisher.

Cover image: prokop / photocase.de
Printed and bound by CPI books GmbH, Birkstraße 10, 25917 Leck, Germany
Printed in the EU.

Vandenhoeck & Ruprecht Verlage | www.vandenhoeck-ruprecht-verlage.com

ISSN 2365-9173
ISBN 978-3-8471-1201-3

Contents

Introduction 7

Chapter One: Becoming bilingual – The experience of emigration in Cournos, Nabokov, Berberova and Shteyngart 15
   1. Cournos: a hard path to bilingualism 15
   2. Nabokov: a multicultural approach to bilingualism 19
   3. Berberova: an unresolved bilingualism 26
   4. Shteyngart: a flight into bilingualism 32

Chapter Two: Migrant autobiographies – Displacement, nostalgia, discomfort 39
   1. Biography and autobiography 39
   2. The problem of integration into the target culture: Cournos 41
   3. Space-time coordinates in Nabokov's *Speak, Memory* 46
   4. Berberova's autobiography and the Russian intelligentsia in Europe . 54
   5. Shteyngart: a modern immigrant's autobiography 58

Chapter Three: Spaces of plurilingual interdialogism 65
   1. The navigation of soundscapes in Cournos's autobiography 65
   2. Geographical and linguistic dislocations in Nabokov's *Speak, Memory* 73
   3. Plurilingualism and entomology 80
   4. The migrant writer as "homo viator" 82
   5. *Look at the Harlequins!* A sequel to *Speak, Memory* 91
   6. Linguistic plays in the paraphrastic mosaic 94
   7. Implicit bilingualism in Berberova's autobiographical short stories . 103
   8. Shteyngart's practice of bilingualism 109

Conclusion 121

Bibliography 127

Index of Names 135

Introduction

In this volume, I will analyze the concept of bilingualism from a psycholinguistic and social aspect, as an existential condition of some émigré artists. Bilingualism is a complex phenomenon, often associated with exile, emigration and second language learning. Different studies have been carried out on bilingualism in the past decades, in order to understand the processes that control the cross-linguistic dynamics and the relationships of interference and communication among the languages employed by bilingual and plurilingual people (Pavlenko 2009, 125; Kroll 2017, 27–28). In particular, I will center on the cases of some Russian-American writers who, after leaving their motherland for the USA, had to tackle the problem of continuing their literary career in another language, English, starting a new translingual phase of their life. In this context, therefore, bilingualism is originated by emigration and the consequent process of cultural resettlement, the latter involving the overcoming of language and culture barriers. However, each of the analyzed writers presents different "overtones" of bilingualism, associated with their experiences. As Edwards (2013, 5) claims, "While almost everyone knows at least a few words in other languages, we generally require a little more competence than that before we are willing to acknowledge bilingual or multilingual ability." Bilingualism, as is known, means being proficient in a second language, and some of the writers discussed in this volume might not have had such proficiency.

Starting from these statements, I mean to point out the difference between explicit and implicit bilingualism, as two different ways to express one's competence in two languages. The former is the ability to speak, write and understand a second language, whose knowledge is explicit in that it is "exemplified" in all its aspects (Grundy and Timmer 2017, 325–326). Nabokov (1899–1977), for instance, one of the writers discussed in this study, epitomizes explicit bilingualism, as he adopts English as his literary language after emigrating to America and even self-translates his works into English. Such explicit bilingualism is revealed in the writer's remarkable ability to "manipulate" his stylistic and lexical choices in the process of translation, thus not always keeping to the source text

(Hetényi 2018, 49–50). Implicit bilingualism deserves, instead, more attention, since its in-betweenness as a linguistic condition is increased by the (assumed) writer's lessened ability to use the target language in all its aspects. As we will see, among the artists analyzed, Nina Berberova (1901–1993) best embodies this concept, owing to the fact that, after her emigration overseas, she did not stop using her mother tongue, Russian, as her literary language, relying on the work of translators to spread her writings in the English-speaking context.

Implicit bilingualism is strictly connected with home-language maintenance, namely the effort to limit the source language attrition by not quitting writing in one's mother tongue (Worthy, Nuñez and Espinoza 2016, 22)[1]. Despite using her source language, Berberova's bilingualism is implicit, in her short stories, in the choice of the characters, themes and settings, where foreign people experience the dramatic loss of their origins, along with a sense of dispossession and non-belonging. By "transplanting" the Russian-speaking characters of her stories in her host country, she preserves their source language, but conveys the immigrants' social and cultural problems and conceptually reproduces a form of bilingualism that is implicit in the characters' circumstances and lives. She exemplifies bilingualism in non-verbal situations. Such bilingualism is abstract and conceptual, as it is not linguistically expressed by the writer, but appears in the characters' interactions with their foreign context. The same concepts of unhousedness and otherness stand out in the form of an implicit bilingualism, in that the foreign characters of the stories do not adapt to their new surroundings, and keep on using their mother tongue. As a consequence, their culture shock is more evident and perceivable, with places and situations where the language barriers alter any form of communication and hinder the process of the characters' adaptation. A writer like Nabokov exemplifies bilingualism in verbal situations, which show a bilingual (and even multilingual) context, where different languages clash. His English works are often interspersed with foreign words and idioms, that become part of the whole target text and interact within its macrotextual universe, thus forming a plurilingual writing. In light of this perspective, explicit bilingualism materializes in the use of foreignisms, in the verbal aspect of the narration that employs words and expressions from different cultural and linguistic universes. However, as we will see, Nabokov is able to create a harmonic relationship among the foreign elements within his macrotext and the sense of estrangement seems, at times, to fade, whereas, in Berberova's works, the contrasts and the problems generated by the language barrier are

---

1 As regards language attrition, Schimd and Köpke (2017, 638) state that "First language (L1) attrition is [...] considered to be the process by which (a) pre-existing linguistic knowledge becomes less accessible or is modified to some extent as a result of the acquisition of a new language, and (b) L1 production, processing or comprehension are affected by the presence of this other language."

more difficult to overcome. Her use of the source language in a foreign context maintains an eternal sense of estrangement and makes the characters' life harsher. Such estrangement is not conveyed by the verbal interaction, as the characters speak the same language, Russian, but is increased by the foreign setting and by the events and situations that occur in their alienating life.

The phenomenon of language attrition is, apparently, more evident in the case of explicit bilingualism; as Laufer and Baladzhaeva (2015, 229) write

> When immigrants learn a new language (L2), use it frequently, and reduce their use of L1, they may experience deterioration in some aspects L1 [...]. As L2 proficiency increases, some features of the L1 system may become modified through the influence of the competing L2 counterparts, and some L1 forms (though not necessarily forgotten) become less accessible than their L2 counterparts.

Language loss is increased by linguistic interferences, borrowings and code-switchings in the sentences of such works as Nabokov's *Speak, Memory: An Autobiography Revisited* (1966)[2], in which the dialogues among the characters abound in words and phrases from different languages. Explicit bilingualism, more than implicit bilingualism, may lead the speaker to lose some structural features of his or her source language and be proficient in the target language. Nevertheless, interaction with foreign contexts increased – more than in the other writers analyzed in this work – so that Nabokov's linguistic competence resulted in the use of frequent puns and sound effects in his autobiographical text (Slavkov 2015, 715). The four Russian-American writers, Cournos, Berberova, Nabokov and Shteyngart, can be analyzed from different perspectives of bilingualism, which develops from its implicit expression in Berberova to its explicit one in the other three writers, in particular in Nabokov's works (Meade and Dijkstra 2017, 49–52). Nabokov, therefore, "inherited" his predecessor's (Cournos's) experience and paved the way for the new generation of Russian-American emigrants, like Shteyngart, representing a model of literary translingualism.

Bilingualism can be considered from a semantic approach as well, since it "juxtaposes" different languages and fosters a comparative study, particularly in *Speak, Memory*, among heterogeneous worlds. Such comparisons highlight the possible linguistic relationships, along with the structural and phonic influences among the languages employed by the four Russian-American writers. The convergence of words within the same semantic field, but belonging to different linguistic contexts, suggests a comparative analysis, which emphasizes the pos-

---

2 According to some scholars, Nabokov's revised autobiography was published in 1966 (Carosso 1999, 18; de la Durantaye 2014, 165; Dembo 1967, 278; García de la Puente 2015, 587; Nafisi 2019, 1; Ponomareff 2013, 403), according to others it was published in 1967 (Connolly 2005, xxii; Cooper 2018, 41; Grayson 2001, 138). In this volume, I will assume that 1966 is the date of publication.

sible similarities and differences among the languages that plurilingual writers employ (Sapir 2007, 192–205). In the bilingual texts discussed in this study, foreignisms are often decomposed, analyzed and compared with their cognates in another language. The words and foreignisms will be examined from the perspective of their meaning and how it changes in accordance with different settings. From a semiotic point of view, bilingualism involves the intersection of space-time dimensions, with the consequent combination of different signs and voices. As I will discuss, the four writers' bilingual texts present different expressions of bilingualism, according to the presence of foreign phrases, words and sentences.

The mixture of cultural and linguistic elements depends on the émigrés' itineraries and on the extent to which their cultural spheres coincided with the places they crossed. When the emigrant writer lands in the host country, his or her cultural world interacts with a new context. The space that is generated by this interaction is the result of a semiotic interchange of signs, sounds, letters and words. The third space, the space where the writer's cultural sphere and the culture of the land of emigration intersect, is the fertile ground where transnational elements take root and form the structure of a bilingual world (Marrone 2018, 154–163). The semiotic elements of the two intersecting spheres produce a bilingual universe, where new forms of communication take place. This space, like any other cultural and linguistic space, can be compared to a living being, whose existence is connected with the presence of other socio-cultural elements. It is dynamic and always in motion, as the elements that it contains clash, mingle and form a new setting of interferences, misunderstandings, communicative acts, cultural disappointments and explosions of new meanings (Lotman 1993, 87–88). The clash of the elements and the explosion deriving from it make this third space more and more unpredictable, in that the phenomena that it produces are subject to the ever-changing nature of the cultural interactions between the two systems. It is within the borders of this space that the contrasts and points of discontinuity between the two cultures stand out, and the meanings that arise change according to the different backgrounds outlined in the plurilingual texts.

Being also travel narratives, the autobiographies examined in this study trace the writers' journeys and map the numerous places of their socio-cultural life. They organize such places into concentric spaces which, in turn, "classify" the places of emigration in relation to their impact on the writers' linguistic development. Using another perspective suggested by Lotman, the spaces, where the interaction among different contexts creates an osmotic proliferation of linguistic and cultural elements, can be organized into two concentric circles. The central one is the dominating semiotic system, i.e. the writer's first linguistic experiences and, therefore, his or her motherland, whereas the surrounding one, which might be called peripheral, stands for the host country (Lotman 1985, 64).

The space of the surrounding circle, unlike the central one, which preserves the elements of the mother tongue and of the source culture, is more flexible and open to absorb new semiotic elements. It interacts with a foreign context, whereas the central circle is more static and holds its original cultural features. It is influenced by the succeeding cultural systems, to form the Russian-American cultural space. The autobiographies analyzed in this volume are both the expression of a linguistic intersection and a relationship among the writers' different contexts, where the source context underlies the entire texts and exerts a linguistic influence over the target context. Although the memoirs are written in the target language (except, as mentioned, for Berberova's *The Italics Are Mine*, 1969), the substrate of the mother tongue constantly "releases" its own linguistic elements which, in their phonic and grammar difference, interact with the ones of the target language and somehow contribute to complete the meaning of the text.

This complex mechanism of transcultural interactions is connected with the learning process of a foreign language, which involves the psychological and neurological aspects of the human being. In this regard, Broca's area plays an important role in the learning process of a foreign language and the different levels of bilingualism in the four Russian-American writers are conditioned by its interaction with the foreign contexts (Moro 2008, 158). As the main center of language elaboration in the brain, Broca's area might have influenced each of the four writers in different ways, according to their different level of bilingualism. Being the point of "collection" and recognition of the foreign "data," this area manages the cultural and linguistic interactions within the thinking structures of the bilingual speaker. What exactly happens in the circuits of Broca's area is not the primary object of this research, but I mean to analyze the effects of such interactions in the above-mentioned writers' works, in particular in their autobiographies. The latter include their writers' innermost thoughts and memories and, having originated from their intimate world, they turn out to be useful documents which bring into focus the processes that forged their bilingualism. The autobiography conjures up the events and the circumstances that, in their apparent triviality, actually determined the bilingual personality and its overtones. Bilingualism is a condition whose origin must be traced back to the speaker's childhood experiences. Hence, the importance of an autobiography lies in the research of those transnational elements that originated from the writers' first international experiences.

The émigré writers that I will analyze, present various levels of bilingualism, but Nabokov and Shteyngart, the "modern Nabokov," turn out to be plurilingual writers, because they can master more than one foreign language, like French and English in Nabokov, and Hebrew and English in Shteyngart. In particular, Nabokov and Shteyngart's plurilingualism emerges in their autobiographies through the various expressions, idioms and phrases in Russian and French

(Nabokov) and in Russian and Hebrew (Shteyngart). Shteyngart's autobiography, *Little Failure: A Memoir* (2014) and Nabokov's *Speak, Memory* contain foreign phrases and sentences that are often analyzed from a phonic and semantic perspective and compared with their English cognates. The autobiographies are not only narrative means written to recollect old memories, but also linguistic "exercises" of writing that the authors use to test their command of a plurilingual text. Plurilingualism paves the way for a pluridiscursive context, which consists in the dialogic comparison among languages, cultures and different social, time and space elements (Bakhtin 1979, 172–173). Nabokov, in particular, by translating some English expressions into French and Russian, creates a dialogue, a discursive relationship among the languages, and tries to single out some possible affinities or contrasts from a phonic and semantic perspective. He even writes a few sentences half in English, half in French or Russian, and this plurilingual approach increases the interdialogic nature of the text.

The combination of different languages originates from the mixture of different time dimensions. Being the stories of the writers' past, the autobiographies become narrative places in which various space and time dimensions evoke languages and cultures from different times. The writers then compare the languages they used to speak during their childhood with their adopted one. The past testifies to the writers' first cultural and linguistic impacts and gradually depicts their process of cross-cultural integration along their itineraries from East to West. The autobiographies are stratified texts and lend themselves to a "diachronic" analysis, which explores the linguistic geology of the works. As a consequence, the analysis of these works is bordered by a vertical dimension, the geological "substrate" of their memories, their past, and by a horizontal dimension, the present time of the authors during their geographical route from Europe to the USA. The autobiographical texts develop, therefore, along two dimensions: a geographical and horizontal one, namely the metaphorical map represented in the horizontal plan of the text, which brings to light the authors' plurilingual background, as it illustrates their different stays in Europe before moving overseas, and a geological and vertical one, since the journey across different countries on a horizontal level conjures up the past memories and the languages associated with them. The horizontal dimension is connected with the vertical one: the more the horizontal route progresses, the more the writers' past is unearthed and is compared with their present. This cultural and linguistic enrichment allows a plurilingual writer like Nabokov to self-translate some of his works. Translation and self-translation, as is known, are very difficult tasks, and Nabokov himself points out that it is essential to have "much talent" and a thorough knowledge of "the two nations and the two languages involved" (Nabokov 1941). As Rothermel (2014, 130–131) claims, "Language is inextricably tied to our notions of self and is the way in which we define and orient ourselves and others within our cultures." Travelling is the way that allows the émigrés to compare their own self with foreign contexts and model it through the international influences it receives.

This introduction poses only a few questions about some émigrés' literary evolution. The work will examine four different cases of Russian émigrés who left for the USA, overarching more than a century. The analysis will follow a chronological pattern, starting with Cournos, one of the first Russian writers who moved overseas in 1891, through Nabokov and Berberova, two different literary personalities who lived in the same years, and, finally, Shteyngart, a contemporary Russian-American writer who, having somehow inherited his predecessors' experiences, is an interesting case of modern plurilingual writer. All four intellectuals wrote an autobiography, and this study will focus on their memoirs as essential documents to analyze their experiences. It will dwell, therefore, on the concept of autobiography too, as the literary expression of the phenomena that often emerge when an intellectual moves to a foreign country. The autobiographies are the most useful documents to study the writers' linguistic evolution and to understand the extent to which foreign cultures forged their bilingual and even plurilingual personalities.

The autobiographies "record" the different steps of the writers' linguistic evolution and illustrate the main moments of their language acquisition. They show the way such writers interacted with a new culture and dealt with the problem of language attrition[3]. The leading author of this study is undoubtedly Nabokov, owing to his fame as the writer of *Lolita* (1955) and, together with Joseph Brodsky, one of the most famous Russian exiles who migrated to America. Among the émigré writers, he is mostly concerned with retracing his linguistic evolution and, consequently, is an interesting case study of bilingualism, plurilingualism and self-translation. Nabokov's autobiography and, from other angles, Cournos's, Berberova's and Shteyngart's autobiographies, propose different cases of bilingualism, plurilingualism and implicit and explicit self-translation, illustrating the writers' different behaviours when they address Russian and American readers[4]. By considering the immigrants' typical phenomena, such as displacement, unhousedness, dispossession, cultural integration and nostalgia, the research will examine how these writers dealt with their emigration and the issues connected with it. Such

---

[3] In this case I used "multilingual" instead of "plurilingual" (which refers to the writer's proficiency in different languages) since I mean to underscore the coexistence of more languages in the narrative space of the text. As to multilingualism, see also Baetens Beardsmore 2008, 4–19.

[4] Takahashi (2019, 2) claims that "One of the most significant differences between the original narrative in the second language (SL) and its translation in the target language (TL) is the audience – whom the self-translator addresses."

aspects can be investigated by means of an attentive analysis of their plurilingual approach in their autobiographies, in order to "map" the linguistic borders emerging in the texts and understand the relationships of coexistence among the languages employed. Although the autobiographical works are mainly "monolingual," other languages, namely the ones the writers spoke during their emigration, appear in the substrate of these texts. The interaction among different linguistic codes, which convey their own cultural world as well, forms such plurilingual autobiographies.

Chapter One: Becoming bilingual – The experience of emigration in Cournos, Nabokov, Berberova and Shteyngart

1. Cournos: a hard path to bilingualism

Some factual and descriptive information about the four Russian-American writers is useful to comprehend the different steps that led them to the adoption of their target language, as well as to map the borders that separate their different linguistic worlds. In spite of their similar experiences, different factors influenced the writers' cultural and linguistic background. Their family's attitude to the target culture, the age at which they left their motherland and the relationships with local people and other immigrants forged, in different ways, the four artists' personalities.

Cournos was born in Zhitomir, Russia, in 1881, an important period marked by historically interesting events. As he writes in *Autobiography* (1935), "I came into the world at a momentous time. Hardly three weeks before, […], Dostoevsky died. The week in which I was born, Alexander II, the Tsar of All the Russias, was assassinated" (Cournos 1935, 3)[5]. He moved with his mother and siblings to Philadelphia in 1891 (Ayers 2011, 355; Satterthwaite 1976, 394) and, at an early age, had to learn a foreign language, not to mention the suffering caused by the new environment, quite discriminating towards an immigrant of Jewish origins like him. Unknown to most critics, Cournos is a paradigmatic personality among the writers who crossed the ocean from East to West in order to find better living conditions and, as such, paved the way for the artists of Slavic (and Jewish) origins who later settled in the USA; in spite of his minor fame, he can be viewed as a model for those intellectuals who looked for a better life overseas[6]. The

---

5 All subsequent quotations from *Autobiography* will refer to this edition; page numbers are given parenthetically in the text.
6 Wanner (2012, 157) claims that "Since the mid-1970s more than 1.5 million Russian-speaking Jews have left the Soviet Union and its successor states. Some of them have become writers in the languages of their host countries, and in doing so they have helped to create a new global genre of what one could call translingual Russian diaspora fiction." According to Espino Barrera (2017, 187), "In the past hundred years, the dramatic increase in the number of exiles

phases of Cournos's bilingualism and trilingualism can be traced through an attentive reading of his autobiographical work, along an itinerary that led him from Russia to America, then back to England, Russia, to finally return to America. Cournos's translingual writing is the product of a long transcultural process that takes place after his emigration to the USA and is different from Nabokov's, Berberova's and Shteyngart's experiences. Many Russian intellectuals who went to America "reacted" to their new bilingual status in different ways. Some of them adopted the target language to write their works, other artists used both their source and target languages and others never stopped writing in their source language[7]. Cournos belongs to the first category of émigré writers. Before investigating his autobiography from a linguistic level, it is important to discuss, in the first part of this analysis, the process that led Cournos along the transitional route from the Russian identity to the American one.

In spite of his early emigration to America and his long stay there, Cournos was still "struggling" with the target language when he was thirty-one, on the eve of his departure for London. As he claims in an article, "Having conceived passion for the English language, of which I had not known a word until I was ten, and aware that I owed something to myself after a schooling which ended at twelve, I had made up my mind to go to England to derive what I could of the nature of English on the soil that gave it sap" (Cournos 1960, 13). During his first years in Philadelphia, the writer was aware of his difficulties with English: "[...] in those days I stammered a great deal, and not alone because of the limitations of my English. My childhood in the Russian woods had simply made me incapable of speech" (70). As he writes in *Autobiography*, the process of linguistic integration is not brought to completion in the USA, where he studied at the local schools. He often compares his life in Philadelphia to the Darwinian struggle for survival, and such a struggle originates from his difficulties with the target language: "[...] Life – [...] – was a fierce struggle, a struggle for mere survival" (111). The language barrier made his life in the host country harsh and his knowledge of English did not improve at all. Although Cournos's English "[...] was very limited" (149) fourteen years after his arrival in the USA, his process of cultural and

---

and refugees forced to seek refuge beyond the linguistic boundaries of their native language has brought about a heightened sensibility towards the loss of the mother tongue and a significant amount of translingual literature. Some authors have chosen to cling to their first language in a new linguistic environment, whereas others embrace the language of their new country for economic, ideological or prestige reasons."

7 Wanner (2008, 662) claims that "Over the past decade several younger writers of Russian origin have achieved literary stardom with books written in French, German, and English. Unlike Nabokov, who began his career as a Russian writer before switching to English in midlife, these authors never published anything in their native idiom. Given that they are using the language of their adopted home countries exclusively, they need to be classified as translingual rather than bilingual writers."

linguistic integration had started for some time, as he had been in contact with some intellectuals, like his stepfather's brother, a learned man, and other people, like the philosopher Slonimsky and the artist Feldman, who was his main mentor in art. Cournos was also a great reader and his readings spanned from English to Russian literature; he even started to write his first articles on art in the journal *The Philadelphia Record* and later managed to overcome his linguistic barrier when he moved to London, a voyage encouraged, once again, by an intellectual, Feldman: "I had been for some time developing two correlated passions: the love of the English language and the desire to go to London. The latter desire was further encouraged by Feldman, who had made a journey to England" (183). His numerous readings, as well as the English articles that he read and his translations from Russian into English were exercises to improve his target language. In spite of the difficulties that he had with English in America, his passion for the language increased over the years, and it was mainly connected with his plan to go to England. In 1912 he set sail for London, where he expected to increase his command of English, owing to the city's lively cultural atmosphere. Before settling in London, he visited some of the most famous Italian cities, like Naples, Rome and Florence, and Paris, where he met many artists. As happened for many émigré writers of the time, Cournos's tour around the main European cities was an important moment for his literary education. And yet, the long stay in the British capital did not suffice to increase his knowledge of English, in that, as he claims, "I could not even speak English properly, as the English spoke it" (218). Among the artists that Cournos met in London, Yeats and Pound were the ones who mostly influenced him. His stays in different parts of Europe, as well as his friendship with the most prominent artists, sowed the seeds of his translingual writing. His increasing competence in the target language is proved by the fact that he was appointed, while in England, to the Anglo-Russian Commission, which was sent to Petrograd in 1917 for political reasons.

Cournos's autobiographical work spans from the first years of his life until the end of the 20s and is entirely written in English, with frequent Russian and Hebrew words. Although the writer kept on admitting his limited knowledge of his adopted language, his stays in the English-speaking countries had an important impact on his linguistic background. He employed his target language to write his books and stopped using his source language, the knowledge of which remained quite elementary and not suitable for writing literary works, owing to his emigration abroad at an early age. *Autobiography*, written in the middle of his literary life, sums up his experiences and outlines his identity. The work is the "record" of the writer's main events. It describes his linguistic development and reveals the extent to which his translingual writing can be effective. Cournos had written other books before his autobiography, such as, among the most frequently mentioned, *The Mask* (1919) and *Babel* (1922), but his autobiographical work represents a moment of reflection on his plurilingual status. By retracing the different phases of his life, *Autobiography* questions the writer's proficiency in using his target language as his literary language. When he moved to America at ten, he could not probably speak and write his source language well and, at the same time, it took him several years to have a good command of the target language. However, Cournos's case is particular since he could not properly speak any language once he moved to America.

Autobiography, like the other autobiographies analyzed in this volume, lends itself to a "synchronic" analysis. It gives detailed and linear information and conjures up the writer's passages from a "synchronic" perspective, since it considers the space-time relationships among the geographical areas he crosses during his emigration, metaphorically "assembling" such areas on a horizontal dimension. The synchronic perspective of the text is, therefore, the horizontal plane of space, which combines, in the present time of the story, different geographical areas and re-maps the writer's route, encompassing Eastern Europe and America, via Western Europe. The text "draws" the linguistic maps associated with the writer's journeys on the horizontal plan that metaphorically composes the structure of the book. On a "synchronic" level, the work illustrates the physical path that repeatedly took the writer overseas (Cournos returned to Russia and to Europe, but died in New York). The concept of "synchrony" is associated with the present dimension of the writer's experience, with the linearity of his route and the linguistic interferences brought about by his crossing different countries. From a "diachronic" perspective, any autobiography is by definition the exploration and the evocation of its author's past, and Cournos's autobiography recalls his life and his linguistic evolution until his years in England, where he improved his knowledge of English. The "diachronic" interpretation of the text is more associated with the memory of the main events that influenced the writer's bilingualism or, better, translingualism, like his relationships with the local people he met in the USA and with the intellectuals in the UK. The intersection of these two dimensions generates a linguistically uniform text, in which English, as the years go by along the "diachronic" level, becomes the vehicular language (although Cournos, as I will discuss, employs Russian and Hebrew lexis too), that is to say, an ever-present language in the author's experience and, consequently, the main element of his "synchronic" dimension, while the source language undergoes a process of attrition, owing to Cournos's early emigration. His background is influenced by American and British cultures. Despite "sharing" a common language, they turn out to be very different, mainly from a sociological point of view[8]. Cournos decides to leave the USA and depart

---

[8] In this regard, it is interesting to read Grosjean's (2019, 17–26) account of his emigration, in which he describes the loss of his source language.

for England in order to find more opportunities for his literary career, and often compares the civilized American life and society to a "[…] jungle of Machines in which the struggle for existence is fiercer than in any jungle created by nature" (88). Such a Darwinian perspective fades out when he arrives in London, where he feels at ease from the very first moment: "No sooner had I put my foot here than I felt strangely at ease and familiar with my surroundings, and had the oddly unaccustomed feeling as of coming home" (197). The "diachronic" overlapping of two same-language cultural systems, the USA and Great Britain, as two systems located at different chronological moments of the writer's itinerary, produces a fairly uniform linguistic system, in which English is the vehicular language. Foreignisms, whose function in the text will be analyzed further on, do not often appear in this context. The first conclusion that we can draw is that *Autobiography* is the result of the convergence of transcultural moments in the writer's life and is an example of a translingual-American work[9].

2. Nabokov: a multicultural approach to bilingualism

Among the four émigré writers analyzed in this research, Nabokov is the most known, mainly for his emigration to the USA and his consequent transition from Russian to English. Such linguistic change has raised numerous questions about his cultural identity, thus opening a debate about his Russianness or Americanness[10]. Some information about his itinerary will suffice to look into his experience as an exile and his passage from Eastern Europe to America. After living in Saint Petersburg, Nabokov had to move with his brother to Crimea in 1917 for political reasons, and, although he was not supposed to be away for long, this journey was a "Foretaste of Exile" (Boyd 1990, 136), as he would never see his motherland again[11]. Nabokov's "course" to an English-speaking country had actually already been "plotted" and he crossed Turkey, Greece and France to land in England in 1919. During his stay in Cambridge, from 1919 to 1922, Nabokov

---

9 According to Finkelstein (2016, 453), translingual Russian-American literature includes "Texts written in English by authors whose native tongue is Russian and / or who actively use both languages in their publications."
10 In a famous interview, Nabokov claimed "I think of myself today as an American writer who has once been a Russian one" (Appel 1967, 20). As to the rediscovery in Russia of the works that had been banned by the Soviet Regime and to the different stages of the Russian emigration, see Possamai 2018, 9–13, and Magarotto 2007, 127–144 respectively. There is a debate among some scholars of American and Slavonic studies, since the former claim Nabokov's American identity and the latter state that he is a Russian writer.
11 After the 1917 February Revolution, Nabokov's father became a secretary of the First Provisional Government in Saint Petersburg and, after the October Revolution, he was compelled to send his family to Crimea for safety reasons (Boyd 1990, 110–135).

was considered a Russian writer and was known as Sirin (derived from the mythological creatures of Russian legends)[12]. Sirin, therefore, is the Russian Nabokov and "[...] the leading light of the younger generation of exiled Russian literati" (Cornwell 2005, 152) who, as an émigré writer abroad, wrote his books in his source language. His literary production in Russian continued during his years in Berlin (from 1922 to 1937) and in Paris (from 1937 to 1940) until his departure, in 1940, for the USA (Boyd 1990, 197–523)[13]. After more than twenty years in Western Europe, Nabokov left for America with his family, and this passage to the New World gave him a completely new identity, which returned to him his real surname, Nabokov, as well as the status of an American writer[14]. In contrast to Cournos, who returned to Europe and to Russia and did not use his source language in his writings, Nabokov never went back to his motherland (but returned to Western Europe and died in Switzerland), and his passage to America marked his permanent transition to English. However, he never completely relinquished Russian and his production includes his English novels, along with self-translations of some of his Russian and American works. This short biographical introduction poses some questions: how did Nabokov's literary background change during his European years? How did Europe influence his writing and his choice of his literary language?

Nabokov's experience deserves particular attention for the ceaseless interlingual dialogue that permeates his American works, in which different cultural and linguistic elements converge and interact to form a narrative translingual *corpus*. His long route from Russia to Western Europe paved the way for the composition of his translingual-American writings, in that he absorbed different semiotic elements from the countries he crossed and achieved a good mastery of French, owing to his stay in France, and became, more than a bilingual writer, a

---

12 Cornwell (2005, 151) writes that "By the middle of the 1930s, Nabokov, writing since 1920 under the pen name 'V. Sirin,' had achieved an enviable reputation as the leading Russian émigré writer of prose fiction." See also Pitzer 2013, 162.
13 Nabokov considered himself a trilingual, however, his knowledge of German may not have been bad because, "Although his mastery of German certainly never approached that of his three essential tongues, his professed ignorance of that language may well have been considerably exaggerated. This probably stemmed in part from a relative distaste for German life and culture [...]. The rise to power of the Nazis made Germany even less congenial, and indeed dangerous, for the Nabokov family" (Cornwell 2005, 153). As Gan (2019, 157) writes, "Between 1921 and 1924, Berlin became the émigré centre of Russian cultural and intellectual life, but also of émigré political and military organizations that tried to resuscitate the White movement abroad."
14 Boyd (1991, 11) describes Nabokov's arrival in New York as the prelude to a new successful life: "On May 28, 1940, the *Champlain* glided through a lilac morning mist past the Statue of Liberty and docked at the French Line pier. After twenty years as stateless Europeans subject to officious bureaucracy at every border, the Nabokovs savoured their arrival in America as an awakening from a nightmare to a glorious new dawn."

trilingual writer[15]. During his European years, he read and studied the main European writers' works, did some translations and wrote his novels in Russian. He translated, for instance, *Alice's Adventures in Wonderland* into Russian (1923) and self-translated into English, in 1938, his Russian novel *Kamera obskura* (1932), whose title became *Laughter in the Dark*. The latter was actually the revision of the English translation by Winifred Roy in 1936[16]. Apart from translating, reading the main European writer's novels and writing his Russian books, Nabokov did not write any novel in English until he published, in 1941, his first English work, *The Real Life of Sebastian Knight*[17]. In Western Europe, the writer could "collect" different voices from the countries where he lived. The European years forged his translingual identity, and provided him with the tools that he would employ to compose his English books overseas. Western Europe stands for his first "mooring," where Nabokov met the members of the Russian intelligentsia and the main artists of the time. Such a context prepares his identity as an American writer, translator and self-translator. Nabokov, therefore, more than a translingual or an American writer, is a translingual-American writer, as he adopted his target language to write his works after his emigration to America, and that language is English.

The linguistic experimentation stands out in his numerous English works, because influences from other languages are frequent. Considering that most of Nabokov's novels are autobiographical, the writing that will be analyzed is his autobiography *Speak, Memory*, published after the revision of previous versions[18]. The "evolution" of Nabokov's autobiography accounts for the different linguistic phases that he underwent. A first English version of his autobiography appeared in 1951 with the title *Conclusive Evidence: A Memoir*, later self-translated, with some changes, into Russian as *Drugie berega* in 1954, and finally retranslated by the author into English, with some further revisions and addi-

---

15 Nabokov (1990, 5) claims "I was bilingual as a baby (Russian and English) and added French at five years of age."
16 As regards Winifred Roy's English version of Nabokov's *Kamera obskura*, Cornwell (2005, 157) confirms that Nabokov was "Deeply dissatisfied with this translation, but anxious not to lose his first English publication, Nabokov agreed with some reluctance to its appearance." Hetényi (2018, 49) writes that Nabokov considered Roy's translation "a superfluous translation of his Russian *Kamera obskura*."
17 In an interview, Nabokov (1990, 5–6) explains what he wrote and translated during his European years, and points out that the first English novel that he wrote was *The Real Life of Sebastian Knight* in 1939 in Paris, then published in 1941.
18 As to the connection between fiction and reality in Nabokov's *oeuvre*, Coye Heard (2016, 145) writes that "[…] Nabokov insists that the escapist artist or reader who denies that there is *any* link between the worlds of fiction and historical experience fails both politically, by abdicating worldly responsibility, and aesthetically, by ignoring the structures that connect the world of the novel to other worlds, including the world of historical, political life."

tional information, as *Speak, Memory: An Autobiography Revisited*[19]. As well as that, as the author writes in the foreword to his autobiography, different sections of his work had already appeared in some American magazines. Such sections are "fragments" of numerous moments in his life, whose "collection" into a single work creates a more linear image of his route. Nabokov's identity is outlined in the three versions of his autobiography, which map and re-map his linguistic evolution from the year of his emigration until his present time. By retracing his life and re-writing it in English, in Russian and again in English, he dwells on the main moments of his childhood and teenage years that forged his transnational personality[20]. In this regard, it is worth quoting what he writes in the foreword:

> This re-Englishing of a Russian re-version of what had been an English re-telling of Russian memories in the first place, proved to be a diabolical task, but some consolation was given me by the thought that such multiple metamorphosis, familiar to butterflies, had not been tried by any human before (Nabokov 1966, 12–13)[21].

By anticipating his linguistic "feat" in the foreword, Nabokov points out that *Speak, Memory* is the product of a "stratifying" process, generated by the continuous revision of the previous versions. Re-writing his life or, better, part of his life, means rephrasing some sentences, adding further autobiographical details and, from a diachronic perspective, increasing the linguistic "sedimentation." *Speak, Memory* is a linguistically layered work, in which the interaction and, sometimes, the combination of different linguistic codes, derives from the author's linguistic emigration.

Set against Cournos's experience, the author's image, constructed by means of his memories and linguistic interferences, should be conceived in a different way. *Autobiography* follows the chronological order of the author's events and mainly focuses on his physical route, as it often dwells on the places where Cournos stayed, although numerous pages linger on his memories and sometimes stop the chronological progress of the text. Cournos's autobiography retraces his past by connecting it with his physical itinerary, as it describes the places and spaces that bring back his memories. It is, therefore, mainly set within the frames of a space

---

19 Nabokov's autobiography was published in 1951 with the title *Speak, Memory* in the United Kingdom and *Conclusive Evidence* in the USA (Nabokov 2016, 634). The peculiarity of this autobiographical "trilogy" is represented by the fact that the revisited version of *Speak, Memory* revises *Conclusive Evidence* and includes the changes made in *Drugie Berega* (Dadashova 2016, 81–82). In this volume, I will analyse the autobiography that Nabokov published in 1966.

20 As Boyd (2011, 265) writes "Nabokov always insisted that audiences needed to know the details of artists' work but had no right to know the details of their lives. True to that principle, he made his own autobiography more a work of art than any other autobiography has ever been, and he left out almost all his adult life."

21 All subsequent quotations from *Speak, Memory: An Autobiography Revisited* will refer to this edition; page numbers are given parenthetically in the text.

dimension that repeatedly takes the writer from East to West. It reads as the account of an itinerary in which the evocation of the memories is connected with the writer's physical route. The journey is the primary theme and "provides" the space elements to conjure up the writer's past. *Speak, Memory* presents a very different narrative structure; being a recollection of memories, the events are not arranged in chronological order, but evoke the writer's childhood by means of proleptic and analeptic devices, linguistic interferences and sudden space-time switchings (Cojocaru 2017, 112). The French and Russian words and sentences that Nabokov quotes in the English macrotext are often associated with the past moments in which he used French and Russian. In contrast to *Autobiography*, which primarily portrays the writer's physical route to "generate" the past memories, *Speak, Memory* offers an opposite structure. It is mainly based on Nabokov's metaphysical world, on his solipsistic dimension, whose surrounding environment is given its own meaning according to the relationship that Nabokov's inner world establishes with it. The text is dominated by the writer's *ego*, his meditations, thoughts and reflections that lead the reader to his most intimate world. As compared with *Autobiography*, it presents fewer references to the space elements that compose his itinerary. As a consequence, the imaginary dimension, the exile's most intimate and immaterial world, overshadows the material elements reflected by the places and by the route mentioned in the text. In the opening of *Speak, Memory*, Nabokov "draws" specific space-time coordinates, because, as he writes, "The present work is a systematically correlated assemblage of personal recollections ranging geographically from Saint Petersburg to St. Nazaire, and covering thirty-seven years, from August 1903 to May 1940, with only a few sallies into later space-time" (9). The very first lines of the work foreshadow a well-organized structure from the perspective of the plot, as the autobiographical story will cover a specific time span and a geographical area, lying between Europe's easternmost and westernmost points mentioned in *Speak, Memory*. However, the narrative space that is included between those years and places is characterized by the anachronistic account of numerous memories and discourses on some aspects of life, whose combination with the places and the people evoked in the text is lost in the "whirlpool" of time.

Time influences the author's linguistic development and evolution as each linguistic phase corresponds to a particular moment of his life. The loss of time, caused by displacement, is the result of the writer's dismay, and stands for a moment of discontinuity, generated, in turn, by the interaction with different linguistic contexts[22]. This interaction produces moments of discontinuity, short

---

22 Ponomareff (2013, 405) states that "It was the loss, the absence, the haunting imagery of a lost world, the sense of emptiness and nothingness – not the loving details of a life remembered – that came to define the traumatic reality in Nabokov's autobiography."

losses of memory, while the writer is absorbed in his thoughts to redefine his identity. Among his intertwined memories, he describes an image, in the opening of the work, which poses questions about what lies before and after our existence. Nabokov means to trace man's linguistic development and opens the autobiography by claiming that our life is a brief moment between two eternal ones, namely what lies before our birth and what lies after our death. The writer claims that "The cradle rocks above an abyss, and common sense tells us that our existence is but a brief crack of light between two eternities of darkness" (19). Moreover, he writes as follows: "Over and over again, my mind has made colossal efforts to distinguish the faintest of personal glimmers in the impersonal darkness on both sides of my life" (20). Nabokov strains to "make out" the linguistic elements that may have predetermined the course of his life in his pre-birth phase. Such predetermination, of chomskyan echoes, is connected with the supposed existence of the two spaces of his conscience before and after life, which complete everyone's existence and form a single path with it. Nabokov tries to grasp the very first moments in his life in order to make out the uniformity of this path. He writes: "In probing my childhood (which is the next best to probing one's eternity) I see the awakening of consciousness as a series of spaced flashes, with the intervals between them gradually diminishing until bright blocks of perception are formed, affording memory a slippery hold" (21). The opening concept of life predetermination, never explicitly expressed, is followed by the use of different linguistic elements, which appear in the text soon after Nabokov's metaphysical discourse comes to an end. His reflections on the metaphysical dimensions that border the beginning and the end of our lives pinpoint the existential "structure" that awaits every man. After recalling the first moments that followed his birth, he recognizes his destiny of a plurilingual man, emphasized by the sudden use of foreignisms to write about his childhood, as if his life had been forged to live in an international context.

Nabokov explains such linguistic predetermination by describing a phenomenon that happens to him every night, before falling asleep:

> Just before falling asleep, I often become aware of a kind of one-sided conversation going on in an adjacent section of my mind, quite independently from the actual trend of my thoughts. It is a neutral, detached, anonymous voice, which I catch saying words of no importance to me whatever – an English or a Russian sentence, not even addressed to me, and so trivial that I hardly dare give samples, [...]. This silly phenomenon seems to be the auditory counterpart of certain praedormitary visions, which I also know well (33).

According to Grayson (2001, 49), "Loss was his [Nabokov's] first theme as an émigré writer, and he trained his memory and his inner eye on the recall of the irrecoverable perfect past. He dreamed of Russia constantly; he recrossed the borders over and over in his imagination, wringing every drop of poetry from it."

The writer's sleep can be compared to his life or, better, his life in another context, and the anonymous voices in English and Russian are the echoes coming from the writer's conscience. His conscience is the image of his pre-existential condition and foreshadows his status of a bilingual from the pre-birth phase. The "trivial" sentences that he "hears" in two languages mark the beginning of his life and, despite not making sense, as he claims, they intertwine to mould his bilingual personality. His complex background belongs to a predetermined design that emerges when foreign words crowd his mind during the unconscious state of sleep, namely the unconscious condition that comes before life[23].

The path of life described in the opening of the book is "re-used" by the author to explain the "evolution" of his existence, characterized by different linguistic and geographical phases. He compares his life to a spiral; in particular, he writes that "The twenty years I spent in my native Russia (1899–1919) take care of the thetic arc," namely "the small curve or arc that initiates the convolution centrally" (275). "Twenty-one years of voluntary exile in England, Germany and France (1919–1940) supply the obvious antithesis," that is to say the antithetic part of the spiral, "the larger arc that faces the first in the process of continuing it;" and "The period spent in my adopted country (1940–1960) forms a synthesis – and a new thesis," the "still ampler arc that continues the second while following the first along the outer side" (Nafisi 2019, 1). The geographical illustration of his linguistic education highlights the writer's assimilation of various linguistic and cultural elements. Such elements, after the synthetic phase, lead him to write his revised autobiography by including those same foreign voices that "crowd" his mind before falling asleep. In this anachronistic narration of his life, Nabokov provides some space-time references. His spiralled itinerary is formed by three specific moments in his life, and each of these moments lasts more or less twenty years. Although all three moments have the same duration, the image of the spiral shows how the arcs enlarge as the years go by, enclosing the ever-changing aspects of reality and enriching the writer's plurilingual experience.

The spiral embodies the qualitative aspect of time, as opposed to its quantitative aspect, represented by the three twenty-year phases. If, from a quantitative angle, the writer's objective experience lasts twenty years in each of the places that he mentions, the qualitative aspect of his spiralling process stands for his inner time, which transcends the objective one and encloses, within its "coils," nu-

---

23 The pre-existent world that Nabokov recalls is part of his imagination as well, because, as Cojocaru (2017, 114) explains, "[...] the mind can grasp the past only with the assistance of imagination. [...] human reason will always have a distorted perception, it is through imagination that the aesthetic value can be registered. [...] The juxtaposition of imagination and science in this device shatters the boundaries between the two, inviting a search for the autobiographical truth outside factual accuracy."

merous a-temporal moments (Swan 2016, 13). In such moments the writer lingers on the different linguistic codes that express some particular events of his life. The writer's present time is set in the antithetic phase, since, as he writes, "For the moment I am concerned with my antithetic stage, and more particularly with my life in Continental Europe after I had graduated from Cambridge in 1922" (275–276). *Speak, Memory* depicts the writer's education *in fieri*. Being in his antithetic stage, Nabokov frequently employs French and Russian words and underlines, in this way, that his autobiography is the "work in progress" of a complex linguistic process. Nabokov "[…] saw language as the essential form of consciousness: memory, love, and life itself. As a result, his surrender to the English language was not an easy one. He had to tame the language, digest it, and turn it into something that belonged to it" (Nafisi 2019, 34). The author often avails himself of foreignisms in the text and in his English works. As a result, he shows that the spiralling process never ends and continually includes new characteristics from other places and cultures. The presence of foreign elements in his English writings helps him to "tame" the target language and to master English by means of foreign signs. The constant interaction with other languages in his autobiography generates the never-ending succession of the three phases, as Nafisi (2019, 44) explains: "The spiral of Nabokov's life and art followed the 'synthesis' of his lifetime, and now, once again, it has found the threshold where he crosses over to a new 'thesis'."

3. Berberova: an unresolved bilingualism

Berberova was contemporary with Nabokov and shares many elements with him. Born in 1901 in Saint Petersburg, she left Russia in 1922 and lived in Berlin first, until 1924, and then moved to Paris, before emigrating to the USA in 1950, about ten years after her compatriot. In spite of the differences that some scholars have remarked between autobiographical memories written by men and women, owing to the fact that the latter "[…] refer to their own and others' emotions more frequently than do boys and men" (Bauer, Stennes and Haight 2003, 27), Berberova's memoirs, *The Italics Are Mine*, retrace her life with the same intensity as Nabokov does, even though Nabokov "sets" his autobiography in his complex world of thoughts and philosophical reflections. Her autobiography, from a narrative perspective, includes both Cournos's and Nabokov's autobiographical features. It contains specific references to the places where she stayed with her partner Khodasevich (who died in 1939) and, at the same time, tells about her life as an émigré and the problems connected with this condition. If Cournos's *Autobiography* gives more objective details, linked to the physical elements of his itinerary (although the writer, as explained, does not omit his comments on the places where he stayed and the people he met), and Nabokov's *Speak, Memory* emphasizes his solipsistic world, which revolves around the "ekphrastic" language of his inner images, Berberova often recalls the places she crossed. At the same time, she gives a portrait of the evolution of her inner world during her emigration. At the beginning of the first chapter, "The Nest and the Anthill," she points out:

> I WOULD LIKE TO WARN THE READER: THIS BOOK is about myself, not about other people; an autobiography, not a set of memoirs, not a collection of portraits of famous (or not so famous) contemporaries, and not a series of vignettes. It is the story of my life, and in it I loosely follow the chronological order of events and uncover my life's meaning. [...] The tale of my long life has a beginning, a middle, and an end. As it unfolds it will become clear where I see its interest and its value. [...] the meaning of life will unfold, the meaning of *my* life, or, indeed, of every life. This meaning [...] will creep into the tale and coexist with time and space, and other things which are on the same level for me as the air [...] I breathe (Berberova 1993, 3)[24].

Like Cournos' *Autobiography*, *The Italics Are Mine*, apart from some flashbacks and flashforwards that "slow down," at times, the storyline, follows a defined design by merging the space-time references. Berberova evokes her route from Russia to the USA, via Western Europe, and the memories connected with each step of her long itinerary. Along this route, which follows a chronological path, the writer portrays the background of her "I," influenced by the relationships with the Russian community in Western Europe.

In spite of Berberova's statement at the beginning of her work, *The Italics Are Mine* is not only a diary about the writer's private experiences as an emigrant, but also an account about her relationships with the people she met abroad. She consequently employs different narrative means, like letters, lists, essays and poems, to make it an "encyclopedic" work on Russian emigration in the first half of the 20th century[25]. In this way, she merges, like Cournos and Nabokov, physical

---

24 All subsequent quotations from *The Italics Are Mine* will refer to this edition; page numbers are given parenthetically in the text.
25 As Peterson (2001, 495) explains, although Berberova claims that her autobiography is about herself and not about other people, she "cannot escape a biographer's voyeurism and transgressiveness when writing about others in relation to herself." *The Italics Are Mine* "[...] is a vibrant, richly textured account of the greatest figures in politics and the arts. It tells us a great deal (but not all) about the author and her strong opinions and judgements of people and events (Barker 1994, 554). In addition, it is interesting to point out that *"THE ITALICS ARE MINE* is a compendious, digressive book more than five hundred pages long. It is like an émigré's travel trunk, fitted with mirrored compartments and secret drawers and stuffed with all sorts of memorabilia and written forms. Among them are: (a) Lists, [...]. (b) Scraps and jottings, [...]. (c) Letters, [...]. (d) Philosophical digressions and meditations. (e) Accounts of Nina's dreams, [...]. (f) Stories of real people's lives [...]. (g) Chunks of quotation from the prose and verse of Russian and European authors. (h) Literary essays and reviews. (i) Two

exile with metaphorical exile; the former is "[…] an expulsion or absence from one's native country against one's will," whereas the latter is "[…] the thoughtful complexity of artistic creation" (Kalb 2001, 141)[26]. The three authors "use" their exile to enrich their background and Berberova, in particular, often comments on many European literary works. Her memoirs become a polyphonic text, which combines voices from different cultural contexts[27]. The three émigré writers construct, in different ways, their creative exile, employing the frustration and the difficulties that it entails to redefine their new cultural and linguistic identities. The themes of exile and homelessness are introduced in the first chapter of her autobiography, titled "The Nest and the Anthill," metaphors for any space that can offer a shelter, a home. From the beginning, Berberova states that her home has never offered her a safe shelter:

> I am the kind of person whose childhood house did not become a symbol of security, warmth, and joy in life, but whose destruction brought me immense jubilation. I possess neither 'ancestral tombs' nor a 'sacred birthplace' to lean on in difficult moments: I never acknowledged blood relationship, […] I have gone on living without support, without weapons, without training in defence and attack, […] not belonging to any political party and not worshipping gods or ancestors. The hardest thing for those like me to accept is that the elements we struggle with are still not formulated: we struggled against enemies that still have no firm shape, […] (72).

Her strong attitude leads Berberova to refuse her relatives' love, to deny her own origins and a place where she can worship her family. Her spirit of independence astonishes the reader, who would expect an exile woman to be asking for support. Her courage stands out when she denounces the Soviet Regime and its repressions against the artists and their freedom of expression:

> At that time in the entire Western world there was not *one single* writer of renown who would have been *for us*, who would have lifted up his voice against the persecution of the intelligentsia in the U.S.S.R, against repressions, Soviet censorship, arrests of writers, trials, the closing of periodicals, against the iron law of socialist realism, any violation of

---

sections of intimate journal […]. (j) Confessions. (k) Veils. Palpable omissions. Pockets of air. Silences" (Fraser 1996, 45–46).
26 In this regard, it is useful to quote what Brodsky (1995, 25–26) writes about exile: "[…] exile is a metaphysical condition. At least, it has a very strong, very clear metaphysical dimension; to ignore or to dodge it is to cheat yourself out of the meaning of what has happened to you, to doom yourself into remaining forever at the receiving end of things, to ossify into an uncomprehending victim."
27 According to Kalb (2001, 143), "An examination of the self Berberova created in her autobiography, poetry, and conversations with others, […] brings out the complex nature of Berberova's creative output. Combined with the reference to the political situation against which Berberova was writing, such an analysis suggests Berberova's firm belief in the potentiality of life-affirming, self-creating exile."

which led to the physical destruction of Russian writers (226. Italics are from the quotation).

She even quotes, in chapter three, titled "Tobias and the Angel," the letter that a group of Russian writers sent from Moscow to the editors of the Russian journals and newspapers abroad. The title of the letter is "TO THE WRITERS OF THE WORLD" (228) and contains the Russian artists' complaints against the repressions of the Soviet Regime. They address their emigrated "colleagues" and beg them "[…] to do what is possible, energetically, everywhere: for the social consciousness of the world to rip away for ever the artful hypocritical mask from that terrible face which is communist power in Russia" (231). In spite of her courageous statements about the Communist Regime, Berberova, in the same chapter, actually discloses her own fears and the problems she has to tackle during her exile. The title of the chapter accounts for her fears, in that, turning to the Bible as a source of inspiration, she compares herself to Tobias and to the Angel, Raphael; Tobias personifies her fear, the insecurity of her existence ("Tobias is everything that is fearful and unsure in me," 210), while Raphael stands for life and the enthusiasm to live ("The Angel, […], is all the rest, which includes the ecstasy of life, the sense of physical health, my equilibrium, my indestructibility […]," 210. Antonucci 2004, 45). The chapter that completes Berberova's passage to the English speaking world is "Not Waiting for Godot." It emphasizes the writer's courage once again, as she decides to leave Paris behind and to emigrate to the USA, unlike other émigré artists who lacked the courage to do so. She decided to abandon the French capital for different reasons, like, for example, the economic difficulties, the lack of "intellectual nourishment" (478) and the fact that she had remained alone:

> […] the impossibility of making a living, the inability to change my profession, and, as they say, [the impossibility] of making ends meet in Paris after the war, was one reason for my departure. […] I remained alone or almost alone in that city, where for a quarter of a century I had lived among friends, among enemies, among friend-enemies, […]. Now no one or almost no one remained, and a vacuum of life lay ahead, individual and as a group (477–478).

The title of this section is emblematic in this regard, since it alludes to the two protagonists of Beckett's work, Vladimir and Estragon who, vainly waiting for Godot, actually deceive themselves. They embody, therefore, those intellectuals who remained in France.

Like Nabokov, Berberova singles out the three steps of her route from Russia to America: "[…] my own country, and the one I had lived in for twenty-five years, and the third to which I was going" (484). The description of her itinerary is particularly important in her autobiography, because she employs the metaphor of the "[…] *seam* binding all my opposites" (484). The three different lands of her route, her motherland, Western Europe and the USA, are united by the *seam*, which is comparable to Nabokov's spiral, the metaphor for his life. The *seam* symbolizes the act of writing as well, as the writer tries to put together, to join, the places she crossed by writing her autobiography. Along the route from her motherland to America, Berberova creates a linguistically uniform space, as she employs her source language. The use of Russian in her autobiography aims to build up contacts with those Russian émigré artists who resided abroad. Once she landed in New York, she met many Soviet artists and this accounts for the steady use of Russian, as a linguistic means that allows her to speak to the Russian émigrés through her work. Her source language has the power to unify the different geographical and linguistic spaces; such linguistic uniformity suggests that "[...] Russia itself can be made mobile, carried over and reconstituted abroad" (Gan 2019, 155) and paves the way for Berberova's return to Russia in 1989, towards the end of her life. Owing to her use of her source language, Berberova can be regarded as a multilingual writer, rather than a plurilingual one. Her multilingualism is due to her relationships with different linguistic personalities; however, this does not mean that she could master different languages, an ability ascribed to plurilinguals. Such multilingualism is connected with the international environments she crossed and with the linguistic geographies of her route, which do not testify to her ability to speak more languages. She writes her autobiography in Russian because of her lack of command of the adopted language.

In her autobiographical text, she underscores another aspect that contributed to her multilingualism: she often mentions the Russian émigré writers and scholars she met in the main European cities of emigration and, among them, the plurilingual Nabokov stands out[28]: "I never told Nabokov my thoughts about him. I knew him well in the 1930s when he began to visit Paris (from Berlin) and when finally, before the war, he settled there with his wife and son" (315)[29].

---

28 The term multilingual refers to the coexistence of different languages (and not to their mutual interaction) in an individual's linguistic geography, whereas plurilingual refers to an individual's skill in speaking more languages. Berberova (311–312) quotes in her autobiography some dates that she saved to meet Nabokov, as a proof of her admiration for him. Berberova's admiration for Nabokov is proved by her high praise for Nabokov's translation skills as well. As Boyd (1991, 490) writes, "Nina Berberova, perhaps the most important novelist other than Nabokov himself to emerge in the emigration, dismisses his claim that his Russian strings had grown rusty." In the section of her autobiography titled "Who is Who," Berberova (567) defines Nabokov as follows: "Russian writer until 1940, later an American writer; former émigré. The greatest writer in the Russian language of this century, and one of the greatest contemporary writers in any language." Pitzer (2013, 99) writes that when Nabokov published *The Defense* (1964), "[...] Berberova later recalled the amazement of reading the first chapters of the novel in Paris and her sudden belief that everything the exiles had lost would live on in Nabokov's work – his literary legacy would redeem their very existence."

29 As to the emigration of the Russian intellectuals, see Livak 2007, 23–44.

Nabokov, whose knowledge of various languages improved as his itinerary progressed, must have exerted a strong influence over her and was a plurilingual model for many émigré writers. As a consequence of his long route, Nabokov is, according to Berberova, "[...] the only Russian writer (both within Russia and in emigration) who belongs to the *entire* Western world (or the world in general), not Russia alone" (316). Moreover, she claims that

> Nabokov does not only *write* in a new manner, we learn from him to *read* in a new way as well. He (like some others) creates a new reader. In modern literature (prose, poetry, drama) he has taught us to identify not with heroes as did our ancestors, but with the author himself, in whatever disguise he may hide from us, in whatever mask he may appear (316–317).

With regard to reading, Berberova brings to light an "innovation" we owe to Nabokov, since he switches the focus from the protagonist of the text to its author. According to her, Nabokov introduces the author's shadow into his texts; he emphasizes, therefore, the autobiographical elements, which he "recomposes" in order to retrace his life from a plurilingual perspective. Berberova follows this approach and looks for her own identity in her autobiography. Although Nabokov never returned to his country, he foreran Berberova's itinerary. After making their acquaintance in Paris, the two émigré writers met in New York[30]. America was the third space of emigration for many European writers and artists, the context of translingual literature. As the third space, America was the place where immigrants' cultural characteristics were forged and influenced by the local background[31]. Having brought her itinerary to completion, Berberova's autobiography can be thus considered a transcultural work, rather than a translingual work, as it crosses different cultures, without using, however, the adopted language or other interfering languages.

Berberova comments on what she sees in America and makes comparisons with the European context. Although the arrival in the new continent meant numerous sacrifices for an immigrant like her, *The Italics Are Mine* expresses the writer's astonishment at the novelties (both good and bad) of the New World. In the sections of the text about the "newly discovered land," Berberova points out a double "layer" that covers the American cities. Seen from above, in a picture, for example, they appear as modern urban conglomerates with ever-shining skyscrapers. However, the inner cities, surrounded by those skyscrapers, unfold the

---

30 As Fraser (1996, 44) writes, Berberova "[...] lived long enough to see her work translated and distributed around the world (like Nabokov) and (unlike him) lived long enough to see it acclaimed and openly sold in Russia itself."
31 Berberova (489) highlights that the USA represented the destination for many European émigrés and mentions, in this regard, Alexandra Tolstoy, "[...] the youngest daughter of the writer. She then was director of an establishment that brought 'displaced persons' from Germany and other countries to the USA."

worst aspects of modernization; as a person, that she names "X," says: "The poverty is terrible. Don't believe the papers. They all lie. Prosperity is only the surface. Inside, deep down, the country is indigent. The Negro problem. Alcoholism. You'll see" (486). Poverty and urban blight coexist with luxury and richness. In this context of contrasts, Berberova is attracted by the "[…] want-ads in a new country, a new city" (487), proof that many job positions are available.

Nabokov's autobiographical account remains "incomplete" and stops in France; Berberova depicts the New World and discloses her astounded comments on its urban and countryside features; when she crosses Colorado, Maryland and Kansas, she is impressed by "[…] space and emptiness in all their power" (511) but, when she visits Florida, she sees "[…] many abandoned houses in the outskirts of big and small cities and villages, and deserted stores, churches, garages, workshops, with a broken door, a cracked window, a balcony hanging over an abyss. […] A thousand abandoned automobiles lie upside down, in a common grave" (516). Like Cournos, who includes his temporary return to Europe in his autobiography, Berberova retraces her itinerary. She returned to Europe ten years after her arrival in the USA and went there again five years later. Such backward itinerary increases the writer's displacement, unlike Cournos, whose arrival in England turned out to be fruitful from a literary perspective (but, as I will explain, his return to Russia was a real disappointment). Paris stands for a "no man's land" to her, since she does not know anyone there and the city becomes a place of memories, almost a museum, where every place has its own history and reminds her of her past. In the final section of *The Italics Are Mine*, Berberova confirms her willingness to preserve her source language and quotes Muratov, a Russian writer, who tried to convince her, at the Luxembourg Gardens, "[…] to abandon writing in Russian and to learn quickly to write in any other language" (526). Her source language, as a voice from the past, connects her present life in the USA with her past and makes her linguistic route uniform, albeit "contaminated" by Anglophone interference[32].

4. Shteyngart: a flight into bilingualism

Being an émigré writer of the technological era, Shteyngart deserves our focus. Born in Saint Petersburg in 1972 from Russian-Jewish parents, he emigrated with his family to the USA when he was only seven. His experience suggests a com-

---

[32] As Kalb (2001, 146) explains, "[…] Berberova in exile, Berberova frightened or confused, is also part of a larger, powerful and life-affirming whole, […], a whole that includes all of life and creativity. […] Just as the past should be assimilated into the living present, individual emotions and suffering must come together as part of a more powerful set, to form a free, creative, and independent whole that will survive to bear witness and move forward."

parison, from a linguistic perspective, with Cournos. Both with Jewish origins, their bilingualism was the consequence of their early emigration. Cournos and Shteyngart had to get used to their sense of foreignness: the former struggled with the target language for many years, the latter "[...] managed to get rid of his Russian accent only at the age of 14" (Maior 2015, 123–124). The use of "only" emphasizes the delay with which he could have a good mastery of English, since his parents did not speak English at home and he did not have a TV set. His autobiography, *Little Failure* illustrates his double route, like Berberova and Cournos, as he often returned to his motherland and, being a living writer, he may return there again. The autobiography is, therefore, necessarily an "incomplete" work, in that it covers the writer's life until 2011, when he returned to Saint Petersburg with his family. Like *Speak, Memory* and, to a lesser extent, *Autobiography*, *Little Failure* is a "[...] cross-cultural migrant's tale" because the writer "[...] likes to pepper his writing with Russian or Russian-sounding words and references" (Bryla 2018, 90). The work is interspersed with "voices" and expressions in Russian and Hebrew, and flash-forwards are frequent, especially in the first part[33]. By recollecting his memories, the writer retraces his itinerary to reconstruct his Jewish-Russian-American identity (Maior 2015, 128)[34]. *Little Failure* begins with a brief look at the writer's American period, just after his graduation. In order to explain the title of his autobiography, he emphasizes the linguistic contamination that soon affected his family after their emigration to the USA: "My mother was developing an interesting fusion of English and Russian and, all by herself, had worked out the term *Failurchka*, or Little Failure" (Shteyngart 2014, 4)[35]. His nickname highlights the problems connected with his identity. His parents called him Failurchka because he gave up becoming a lawyer, as they wanted him to be, and took up writing. Failurchka foreruns the difficulties, the failure of cultural integration into the land of capitalism, in the years of the Cold War.

In his work, Shteyngart shows his efforts to understand the cultural symbols that stand out in his hometown. The chronological narration and the description of the writer's education start from the fourth chapter, titled "Moscow Square," a square in Leningrad, where he used to go as a child, and whose architectural features are majestic: "Moscow Square. *Moskovskaya Ploshchad.* This is where my life really begins. [...] Moscow Square: Its geometry is cold, its colors are

---

[33] Brauner (2017, 1) underlines that *Little Failure* is "[...] the narrative trajectory of a Bildungsroman."
[34] Bryla (2018, 1) writes: "At once humorous and sad, the book is a three-culture Bildungsroman illustrating the author's early life in the US and then the road which has led him to becoming one of the most popular ethnic American authors."
[35] All subsequent quotations from *Little Failure: A Memoir* will refer to this edition; page numbers are given parenthetically in the text.

muted, its size is gigantic, and there are occasional colonnades and assorted Greek flourishes to make the place seem timeless and inevitable" (46). His childhood place, Moscow Square, conveys timelessness and displacement even at home. Owing to such a sense of estrangement at home, the emigration to America is the *leitmotif* in the first chapters, since Shteyngart often mentions it in the text, as if he wanted to skip his early years and focus on his American life[36]. In the opening of his work, he recalls the main symbols of the Soviet Regime, like the subway, the statues, the buildings and the numerous allusions to Lenin, which dot the city. The first section of the book conveys the paralyzed atmosphere of the city and the departure overseas foreshadows remarkable changes in the writer's life. The journey to the USA covers different parts of the autobiography and Shteyngart introduces it by describing the circumstance that allowed his family to emigrate:

> Unbeknowst to me, the Soviet Union is falling apart. [...] Meanwhile, in the United States a grassroots movement to free Soviet Jews from their polyester captivity has gained momentum. And so, the American president Jimmy Carter has reached a deal with the Russians. In exchange for tons of grains and some high technology, presumably television sets that won't explode with such regularity, the USSR will allow many of its Jews to leave. Russia gets the grain it needs to run; America gets the Jews it needs to run: all in all, an excellent trade deal (62).

Shteyngart dwells on the weeks that precede his family's departure: "My parents have surrendered their jobs, [...] and are using the remaining rubles to ship our glossy Romanian furniture [...] across the Black Sea, across the Mediterranean, across the Atlantic, across any body of water that will float this strange, superannuated cargo" (62). The ocean is the symbol of timelessness and the moments of discontinuity along the writer's route, those same moments connected with the loss of time in Nabokov's autobiography. The moments of discontinuity pervade the writer's linguistic and cultural evolution. They interrupt the linearity of his cultural route and are "a-temporal" spaces, in which his identity appears as an entity *in fieri*, since it is constantly "re-contextualized" and renegotiated[37]. Like the previous émigré writers, the passage to America was not direct, because the Shteyngarts had to stop in Western Europe. This time, however, the means of transport is different and the long voyages that characterized, for example, Nabokov's passage from Crimea to England are replaced by the short flight to East Berlin. The writer's first flight seems to take him to an unknown place, and the

---

36 As Genette (1976, 115–127) writes, the prolepsis anticipates the events. In *Little Failure*, Shteyngart uses the proleptic device to hint at his emigration overseas.
37 The émigré writers' identity is "[...] the result of an on-going series of transactions between self and community and of repeated attempts in a long process whereby one's self perceives information drawn from experiences of one's own, and evaluates them and himself/herself accordingly" (Maior 2015, 125).

wait becomes more and more exhausting: "Which is *where* again? Mama and papa remain silent and worried throughout the flight. [...] We land with a proper thud somewhere and taxi to a terminal" (80–81). East Berlin airport is the first frontier where Shteyngart perceives a different atmosphere: "East Berlin is the socialist showpiece of the entire Warsaw Pact, and the airport waiting lounge seems to hover somewhere between Russia and the West. There are dashes of chrome, [...] and exotic nongray colors, purple or mauve perhaps" (81). Despite belonging to the Soviet Empire, East Berlin shows some Western influences. Before flying to Vienna from Berlin, Shteyngart is thrilled by the curiosity to see a different world: "Momentarily, we will land in a world unlike any we could have imagined, the one many will tell us is free. But nothing is free" (82). The writer points out that the stages of the itinerary are the same for all emigrants: Moscow, Berlin, Vienna and Rome[38].

The Austrian capital is the first city that Shteyngart sees in the Western world. The writer, still a child, is enchanted by the shop windows and the good services of the city, although he suffers from culture shock and does not hide his feelings of nostalgia: "There are thousands of us Soviet Jews stomping our way through Christmas Vienna that night, mouths agape, letting the pleasure and the horror of home-leaving finally wash over all of us" (84). The writer's family is ready to cross another border and they go to Italy by train. During his long journey to Rome, Shteyngart becomes familiar with the symbols of the country through its colors: the Alps that separate Austria and Italy are green and the Mediterranean sea is blue. During their five months in Rome, the Shteyngarts enjoy the museums, the churches and the historical beauties of the Vatican. At the same time, the writer is more and more aware of the fact that life in his country was being made more enchanting by the Regime than it really was:

> My father [...] tells me what he knows. It was all a lie. Communism, Latin Lenin, the Komsomol youth league, the Bolsheviks, the fatty ham, Channel One, the Red Army, the electric rubber smell on the metro, the polluted Soviet haze over the Stalinist contours above Moscow Square, everything we said to each other, everything we were.
> We are going to the enemy.
> "But, Papa, the Tupolev-154 is still faster than the Boeing 727?"
> In a resolved tone: "The fastest plane in the world is the Concorde SST."
> [...]
> "It is flown by British Airways and Air France."
> "So. It means. You're saying..."
> We *are* the enemy (93).

---

38 As to the immigrants' itinerary, Schwartz (2014, 72) writes: "Shteyngart's energetic memoir follows the arc of most immigrant stories. The newcomer arrives, bewildered and apprehensive, burdened with baggage from home."

During his stay in Italy, Shteyngart finds out through his father's words that the enemy is not the West, as they had always been made to believe at home, but is their motherland, that is to say the place where they are supposed to have a home and a job. Italy is the country where the writer is influenced, for the first time, by the Western world, which prevented him from becoming a *homo sovieticus*; this process is sharper owing to his long stay in Italy. Placed in the middle of the passage from the former USSR to America, Italy discloses a different perspective of the world, it is the place of reflection, where the author reveals the numerous lies of the Regime. The "middle space" separating the two superpowers once again plays an important role in the mediating process between his Russian identity and the American cultural context. It is the semiotic space, after Germany and Austria, where the writer interacts with the signs and the language of a new cultural and linguistic context. The writer is familiar with the Italian culture through the messages and sounds he hears in a foreign language, the advertisements in the streets, the body language, and other forms of verbal and non verbal communication[39]. The "imprint" of the Italian context, as the most important cultural space where the writer's Russian identity interacts with a new world, is symbolized by the Alitalia aircraft, which takes the Shteyngarts to New York JFK. The airline "preserves" the Italian influences as far as the United States and is the Shteyngarts' "cultural brand" until their arrival in the New World. During the flight, Shteyngart becomes aware of his final destination as soon as a stewardess gives him a map of the world: "Here is the vast red terra incognita of the Soviet Union, and there is the smaller blue mass of the United States with its strange Floridian growth on one side. Between these two empires lies the rest of the world. [...] We are approaching the last twenty years of the American century" (94). He can follow the passage to America on the map and make his first personal comparison between the two most powerful countries in the world: on the one hand, he is leaving behind his motherland, which he sees as a "terra incognita," an unknown land, since his father's observations had questioned the reliability of the Soviet principles and made it a strangely unfamiliar world; on the other hand, he is about to land in the USA, whose high buildings that he sees in New York symbolize "the future" (94).

The comparison between the Soviet Union and the USA continues just after Shteyngart lands at JFK airport. The writer uses a "chromatic" metaphor to emphasize the opposition between the flatness of life in his native country and the multiple aspects of the American world: "1979. Coming to America after a childhood spent in the Soviet Union is equivalent to stumbling off a monochromatic cliff and landing in a pool of pure Technocolor. [...] Oh, that immense

---

39 Lotman (1985, 78) explains that signs are essential to communication, whose effectiveness depends on the complexity of the semiotic systems used by the speakers.

solidity!" (95). The monochromatic world of the Soviet Union is in contrast to the multicultural and contradictory reality of the USA. Shteyngart highlights the most attractive aspects of his host country and people's wealth. However, the integration into the new culture is not easy at all, as his descriptions of the country prove: "[…] a complex, media-driven, gadget-happy society, whose images and language are the lingua franca of the world and whose flowery odors and easy smiles are completely beyond me" (104). When Shteyngart recalls his years at the Jewish school, the Solomon Schechter School of Queens, he "[…] takes his identity formation to the extreme: emigration forces his protagonist to negotiate not just his Russianness but also his Jewishness against acquired Americanness. This in turn entails physical and metaphorical movement across spatial and temporal dimensions" (Bryla 2018, 93).

America is the final multicultural context where Shteyngart forges his three-time hyphenated identity: Jewish-Russian-American. Although Italy has a strong impact on the writer's semiotic background, his Western European influences fade as soon as he arrives in America. However, the displacement caused by the American language and culture leads him to his past. The author often describes, in the text, a game he used to play with the map of the world and a toy plane: "When I feel sad from Hebrew school, I turn to my Soviet atlas and an Eastern Air Lines, […]. Using my atlas, I plot out the flight time to Rome, then to Vienna, then to East Berlin, then back to Leningrad" (107). His "itineraries" then became more complex and he "flew" his plane to Leningrad via Paris, Amsterdam, Helsinki, and then via London, Amsterdam, Warsaw and Moscow. Shteyngart is clearly nostalgic for his motherland since he often imagines his return to Leningrad[40].

The writer has to face new problems in the USA, like his relationship with the African American community and the prejudice of the local people against communism and Russians, especially at school. The latter is the first place of interaction with American students, where his identity is questioned and forged by means of the cultural clash he undergoes. As the author goes on telling about his years at the Stuyvesant High School in New York and at Oberlin College, he mentions Nabokov, which proves that Shteyngart had read at least some of his writings. Among the main historical people of the time mentioned in the text, like Bush, Gorbachev and Yeltsin, Nabokov stands out. When Shteyngart organizes a college party in his room and the students lift him onto their shoulders, he asks

---

40 As regards the depiction of the immigrant in Shteyngart's works, Friedman (2004, 79) writes that "[…] the immigrant character does not have to view Americanization as a definitive, totalizing act—nor does he want to do so. He can remain ambivalent about his status in America without fully embracing acculturation […]. Shteyngart's protagonist is indeed a self-proclaimed 'beta immigrant,' a second-class citizen who has not been able to realize the 'American Dream' of wealth and personal success."

himself the following question: "[…] am I thinking of the book I have just read – Nabokov's *Speak, Memory* – in which Vladimir Vladimirovich's nobleman father is being ceremonially tossed in the air by the peasants of his country estate after he has adjudicated one of their peasant disputes? Yes, that is precisely what should be on my mind" (261). One of the characters of the stories that he writes is named "*Vladimir*" (294). Moreover, when he recalls a hot day, he says "And outside it is warm either in the fading way of fall or the rapturous, tenuous way of spring. […] a mirror of some earlier time and place – summer break, North Carolina – that should have pleased the early Nabokov so" (302). These quotations prove Shteyngart's knowledge of Nabokov's works and of his personal life. Nabokov is an example of integration or, better, of steady integration into the ever-changing linguistic features of the American context. The spiralling model of his life shows that any emigrant who moves to the USA constantly interacts with a plurilingual society. The succession of the thesis, antithesis and synthesis enriches his linguistic experience. The emigrant's existence can be compared to the Darwinian struggle, where those who can master more than one language are fitter to live in the plurilingual environment of the New World. Shteyngart needs to become a perfect bilingual to be able to adapt to his new linguistic context.

Like Cournos and Berberova, Shteyngart returns to his motherland but, unlike them, he returns there many times: "Since my first return to Russia in 1999, I've been back almost every other year, dutifully taking down everything I see" (323). In *Little Failure*, he returns to Russia in 2011 as a real American and realizes his difficulty in articulating the Russian sounds. He claims that Saint Petersburg, now with a new topography and very different from the years of his childhood, is still "[…] a sad place. Its sadness lies in a mass grave in its northeastern suburbs along with the 750,000 citizens who died of hunger and German shelling during the 871-day siege" (328). Shteyngart highlights the disappointment generated by his return to Russia and concludes his autobiography in the oblivion of history, represented by the streets of Saint Petersburg, the "vestiges" of the past, and by the cemetery where he visits his grandfather's tomb. The author's choice to end the account of his life in the Russian city, in spite of its sad background, symbolizes his nostalgic feeling and his sense of displacement.

Chapter Two: Migrant autobiographies – Displacement, nostalgia, discomfort

1. Biography and autobiography

Biographies, as is known, underlie any artist's work and require an in-depth study of the documents they contain. Their reliability depends on the quality and the quantity of biographical sources. The truthful aspect of the biography may fail in the autobiography, since the author who writes about his or her own life tends to tell the events from a subjective perspective. The writer's emotional status can affect his or her writing and, unlike the documentary and factual nature of the biography, the autobiography can result in a more fictionalized work[41]. In light of these considerations, to what extent can a reader rely on the autobiography? The four autobiographies analyzed in this volume (and, in particular, *Speak, Memory*) present a particular narrative structure, with numerous anachronisms, like prolepses and analepses (Genette 1976, 96–127). The space-time manipulation allows the authors to "forge" their narration and to present it from a more personal outlook. Autobiographies can be regarded as fictionalized writings from the perspective of time manipulation, since their authors manage the organization of the events they tell according to the importance they had in their lives. The authenticity of the events is, therefore, conditioned by the order and the "narrative" style with which they are presented and by the imprint they left in the authors' lives. However, owing to the subjective perspective of the facts they tell, autobiographies may be the most truthful documents and turn out to be even more reliable than biographies. The latter, being written by someone else, can contain factual mistakes or authorial assumptions that do not mirror the artist's life. The personal perspective of autobiographies makes the reader better

---

41 In his discussion about fictional and factual autobiography, Tlustý (2012, 181) points out that the assumed lack of objectivity of the fictional autobiography "[...] does not mean that we cannot consider the potential correspondence between fictional and real events." de Man (1979, 920) writes that any autobiography "[...] may contain lots of phantasms and dreams, but these deviations from reality remain rooted in a single subject whose identity is defined by the uncontested readability of his [or her] proper name."

sense the author's view of the world and his or her way of living the main social and historical events[42]. Writing an autobiography implies a particular effort of "splitting" one's self and making it objective, by trying to look at the other half of the self and at its surroundings with an impartial perspective, as an eyewitness. This process of "alienation," as Todorov (1990, 136) explains, includes two elements: empathy and abstraction. Empathy is important since the autobiographer needs to adapt to the surroundings of his or her life events. Accordingly, the author investigates his or her environment with the curiosity that is required to grasp the meaning of reality, even when it discloses unpleasant memories. Empathy helps the author to recollect the past in "tranquillity" (to recall the task of romantic poets). As to abstraction, the autobiographer must be able to "catalogue" the facts that he or she means to tell, by arranging the memories according to the filters of the mind. The author can establish a relationship of exotopia with the environment, "split" his or her self and look at it from the outside, as the root of the word suggests (*Ibid.*). Writing about oneself entails a process of separation from one's self, which generates a distinction between the self, the "bodily identity," and the subject, the consciousness (Barreras Gómez 2015, 102). By means of this split, the self can explore the physical world, in its phenomenic essence, while the consciousness reorganizes the author's memories.

The truthful essence of the autobiography is proved by Berberova's *The Italics Are Mine* as, among the messages suggested by the title, it is a text in which every word seems to be directly uttered by the author and, therefore, written in italics. Likewise, any autobiography is a text whose content is not filtered by anyone and is entirely written by its author. In the first chapter, we analyzed the four writers' most important biographical elements: having undergone many vicissitudes, they decided to write about themselves to retrace their background, along with the elements that moulded their personalities. Their autobiographies are, therefore, examples of *Bildungsroman*, since they focus on their authors' process of maturation along an itinerary that led them abroad. By reconstructing their past, these writers look into the ontological meaning of their experiences, in which their *ego* constantly tries to ascribe a meaning to their past events (Bellini 2000, 81). Their autobiographies are the "epistemological" means to understand themselves (Kuek and Ling 2017, 285), as they contain the linguistic and cultural elements of an epoch, which are analyzed in accordance with the writers' experiences. What makes them particular, however, is their plurilingual aspect and the

---

42 Kuek and Ling (2017, 284) define autobiography as a literary genre and claim that "An autobiography is a self-written account about a person's own life. Different from biographies, which are accounts of other people about a person, autobiographies are the biographer's own account. Based on one's vivid memories of one's life, significant people such as politicians, social advocates and other high impact personalities produce autobiographies to expose their selves, along with their reflections on events and people during their era."

use of literary devices in more than one language. They reflect their authors' plurilingual identity and, as such, aim to tell their events by evoking the languages that these authors were using when those events occurred[43]. As a consequence, the space-time chronology often fades and the texts become the "sedimentation" of memories from different linguistic worlds. The numerous foreignisms in the texts, in the form of "fragments" or phrases, conjure up the authors' past. In this regard, the autobiographies entail the "philological" reconstruction of the writers' linguistic background. They are, each in different ways, plurilingual or, better, translingual works, because they employ, with the exception of *The Italics Are Mine*, the target language and frequent foreignisms.

In light of this, autobiographical writing means taking up a self-discovery journey through the different phases of life, as well as reconstructing one's identity with the impartial eye of time. In their autobiographical works, Cournos, Nabokov, Berberova and Shteyngart linger on their plurilingual maturation and on their integration into foreign contexts. Their integration developed in different ways, according to the social and the historical background of the places where they lived; all of them, however, had to tackle the problems connected with language and social barriers. Cournos and Shteyngart center on the problems generated by their Jewish origins before and during the Cold War. Nabokov mainly focuses on the linguistic issues and the metalinguistic relationships among the languages he uses. Berberova shows her concern with the processes of integration of the Russian communities abroad and the development of Russian culture in these "enclaves" as a form of transculture.

2. The problem of integration into the target culture: Cournos

In his memoirs, Cournos never hides the problems he had when he emigrated to America and often makes comparisons between his native country and the American cities. Such comparisons are based on the opposition between a natural, paradisiac world, that is his family farm in Boyarka, a village near Kiev, and the American cities. He claims that "There were no factories in the neighbourhood. I was quite aware of what a factory looked like" (13). The memories of his childhood in the Old Continent are tinged with descriptions of Wordsworthian echoes and, despite a destitute life, he has a romantic view of his past: "Sad my childhood certainly was, but at least it was a lyrical sadness. Nothing incompatible in that. There was autumn with its falling leaves, [...] There was

---

43 Owing to the plurilingual structure of the autobiographies analyzed in this study, it is necessary "[...] to push the book toward abstraction, toward doubleness, toward seventeen types of ambiguity" (Shields 2009, 152).

winter, with its snows, [...] There was the whistling of the wind [...] There was the howling of wolves audible in the winter night" (33). The first disappointment with the "civilized" world comes to light when the writer arrives in the USA: "[...] the rows of small red-bricked houses stretching into infinity through rectilinear streets, monotonously depressing" (61–62) are in contrast to the vast plains of his countryside home in Ukraine. Cournos employs the image of the spaces to underscore the contrast between the rural life in Boyarka and the alienating life overseas. Referring to his birthplace, he says that "[...] my being was fresh from unspoiled woods and sensitized by them [...]" (62). As regards his life in America, he writes: "As a child I *felt* this discord between myself and the mechanized, materialized community, productive of poverty, of slums, of spiritual sloth" (62). The writer's adaptation is hindered, first of all, by aesthetic factors, which make Philadelphia an unwelcoming city, and where the effects of capitalism are visible in the depersonalization of mankind. The sight of the slums and the first interactions with African Americans increase his sense of displacement and he lives as a maladjusted boy, especially at school: "[...] my sylvan past intervened to make life an ordeal. To be plunged all at once among a multitude of boys and girls after one has starved in a practically companionless desert is like being offered a meal after a long fast" (69).

Cournos's suffering from space dislocation stands out in his comments on the buildings and the streets around him. The writer has to undergo the "law of the geographical space," which is a consequence of the uprooting from his "native soil" and of the emigration to a place he does not belong to[44]. He realizes his dislike for the urban atmosphere of the American context. The opposition between the space of his motherland and the space of the American city has an effect on his time dimension, in that it generates a further opposition between the past, his native country, and the present. Cournos's autobiography develops along an "earthly" dimension, because it contains many references to the physical spaces he crossed. The reconstruction of such spaces accounts for the linear and chronological organization of the text. Following the structure of the *Bildungsroman*, *Autobiography* shows that each place along the writer's itinerary refers to a specific phase of his life: Russia represents his childhood, America his years as a young man and the problems connected with integration, England his "literary redemption" and, finally, Russia, again, on his temporary return as a translator, his attained status of a respectable learned man. The importance of the space dimension is emphasized, as explained in the first chapter, by the numerous references to the Darwinian law, whose principle of the survival of the fittest is based on the presence of natural environments, as spaces of struggle among different living beings. In accordance with the sociological trends of the

---

44 For further details about the concept of geographical space, see Hoffman 2011, 11–74.

time, Cournos applies such principle to the urban environment, where the struggle for survival is ruthless, especially when it comes to job hunting: "I was in a jungle, I did find myself *inferior* in a sense to the beasts with stronger teeth and claws than I had; teeth and claws which I sometimes envied, since I lived in a society in which it was hard to do without them" (132). Philadelphia is the first geographical setting where Cournos has to interact with a different culture and to defend himself from social prejudices. It is the space of emigration and modern life, in which he needs to adapt to new circumstances and habits and undergoes bullying episodes because of his origins.

The imaginary interaction among the spaces of emigration is produced by the intense nostalgia for the writer's childhood spaces. The past lies in the "nucleus" of the exile's semiosphere, to mention Lotman, in its inner part which is not changed by the introduction of outer elements. Such elements, in fact, can only interact with the edge of this semiosphere, the immigrant's sign system, but cannot change its deepest layers since they have "settled" as time went by[45]. In its different overtones, nostalgia is mainly a state of steady longing due to the loss of something or someone, like a place or a person. It involves the inner dimension and allows the writer to travel throughout his imagination, in order to return, by means of memory, to those places, times, people and parts of himself that form his individual space[46].

The concept of nostalgia is an important aspect in this and the other three autobiographies analyzed in this volume and, as such, deserves particular focus. Nostalgia tends to "retrieve," to make up for what has been lost and, therefore, can be restorative and reflective (Mirabelli 2012, 5–7). The former consists in the reconstruction of one's home in the host country. Typical examples are the numerous Chinatowns in the biggest American and European cities, as they reproduce "parts" of China in a foreign land, or the emigrants' houses or flats, whose furnishings hardly ever lack the style and the smells of their native countries. Restorative nostalgia tends to recreate the immigrant's birthplace in a foreign land, an artificial space or, in other words, a heterotopic space, namely an

---

45 As Brodsky (1995, 29) writes, "Whether pleasant or dismal, the past is always a safe territory, if only because it is already experienced; and the species' capacity to revert, to run backward – especially in its thoughts or dreams, since there we are safe as well – is extremely strong in all of us, quite irrespective of the reality we are facing. Yet this machinery has been built into us, not for cherishing or grasping the past [...], but more for delaying the arrival of the present – for, in other words, slowing down a bit the passage of time."

46 According to Boym (2011), "[...] nostalgia appears to be a longing for a place but is actually a yearning for a different time – the time of our childhood, the slower rhythms of our dreams. [...] nostalgia is a rebellion against the modern idea of time, the time of history and progress. The nostalgic desires to obliterate history and turn it into private or collective mythology, to revisit time as space, refusing to surrender to the irreversibility of time that plagues the human condition."

"imperfect" reproduction of an unattainable world[47]. On the other hand, reflective nostalgia is a constant feeling of loss that takes the exile back in time. If restorative nostalgia entails the material reproduction of the elements that recall or look like the source culture, reflective nostalgia is based on the imaginary dimension of memory.

The exiles who express reflective nostalgia are aware that their past cannot be retrieved and that, somehow, it does not exist anymore. Unlike restorative nostalgia, which "clings" to the past by collecting its objects to reconstruct the immigrant's lost world and, therefore, avoids resignation, reflective nostalgia expresses an unusual love for the distance from an irretrievable past. It is the result of a mental alienation, a separation from the birthplace (Giorcelli 2008, 10–11). By comparing the urban spaces in the USA with the ones where he grew up, Cournos realizes that even an approximate reconstruction of his childhood spaces is not possible and that what he yearns for belongs to the past. He is thus obliged to content himself with his imagination and "see" his childhood places by relying on his reflective nostalgia. The memories of his birthplace and the Sylvan plains reproduce a heterotopic space, whose immaterial essence lies in the writer's imagination. His home space is a "counter-space," an "elsewhere," an unreal dimension.

In spite of his declared reflective nostalgia and the reveries recalling the places of his childhood, Cournos's narration of his visit to Russia, in the last sections of *Autobiography*, does not reveal the image he was expecting. Cournos, as explained before, grew up in a rural area and was not familiar with the urban context of his motherland. When he went to Petrograd, the modern Saint Petersburg, he saw a new world, what we could call his fourth space, after Russia, the USA and England. Unlike the urban spaces in the USA, where poverty acts as a background to the rapid economic growth, the Russian city presents a "gloomy" atmosphere and many people live in poverty: "[...] there were the queues, the endless queues, waiting for bread, for candles, for lamp-oil, for soap. They stretched for long blocks, these patient queues of men, women and even children, [...] waiting their turn, which often never came, because the supply of the needed article was in the habit of becoming exhausted" (306–307). The four spaces of emigration have different features: the romantic landscapes of rural Russia, the

---

47 About heterotopias, Foucault (1986, 24) writes as follows: "There are also, probably in every culture, in every civilization, real places – places that do exist and that are formed in the very founding of society – which are something like counter-sites, a kind of effectively enacted utopia in which the real sites, all the other real sites that can be found within the culture, are simultaneously represented, contested, and inverted. Places of this kind are outside of all places, even though it may be possible to indicate their location in reality. Because these places are absolutely different from all the sites that they reflect and speak about, I shall call them, by way of contrast to utopias, heterotopias."

social contrasts of the American cities, the vibrant atmosphere in England, France and Italy, whose main cities attracted many émigré artists, and the backwardness of urban life in Russia. His reflective nostalgia, therefore, conjures up the marginal areas of his country, where the environment is suitable for a *bon sauvage*. Travelling forges the writer's experience and his relationship with foreign cultures. Owing to his cultural ambition, he manages to settle into the British context and to overcome the problems caused by discrimination. Although the autobiography does not complete his route back to America from Europe, Cournos chooses to live in the USA, where he partly completes his process of integration, as he explains towards the end of his account: "And again I dream that America, safe between two oceans, has taken it all over, has taken the place of Europe. America can become a great country. America is a better country since the Depression. It is harder to exist – for you and me. Yet it is a better country" (343).

The disappointment that ensued from his temporary return to Russia with the British board was caused by his nostalgia, which made him idealize the image of his motherland as the years went by, thus turning the bad memories of his past into carefree moments of his childhood: "With the passing of years the pity recedes, takes its place as a single component in a pattern bearable because it is a thing remembered, and all such memories are sweet. To have gone through hell and survived without embitterment is not exactly the sort of thing to boast of; nevertheless there is acute pleasure in the thought" (78. Affuso 2012, 112). The return to Petrograd unveils a bleak aspect of his motherland. However, his experience in Europe, where he made acquaintance with the main *literati* of the time, like Pound and Yeats, would ultimately help him to settle in America. Western Europe, therefore, was the cradle of his literary background, the space where he was influenced by foreign cultures.

Cournos's process of adaptation was not easy at all and, in fact, he partly completed it. The writer quotes derogatory sentences by which some criminals addressed him, like "You dirty sheeny!" (68), he is repeatedly robbed in the streets and everybody makes fun of him at school for the clothing he wears. From an anthropological perspective, the process of integration lends itself to different theories, which are relevant to Cournos's case. In his studies about the relationships among different cultures, Todorov singles out three approaches to foreign cultures (2014, 225). The axiological approach is based on the distinction that the emigrant makes, in the adopted country, between good people and bad people. The praxeological approach examines the relationships between the emigrant and the people of the adopted country; such a relationship can be characterized by the emigrant's assimiliation into the new culture or, on the contrary, by the emigrant's lack of integration. Finally, the epistemological approach focuses on the emigrant's knowledge of the culture of the adopted country and the extent to which such knowledge can help him or her to settle into the new culture. The three approaches underlie the relationships among different cultures and it is important to employ them to overcome any cultural barrier.

Cournos's case includes all of these approaches in different ways since, during his first months in the USA, he did not meet any good people and, from an axiological perspective, he disliked Americans. As I have explained, the people the writer met in the USA often looked down upon immigrants. As regards the praxeological approach, the writer's relationship with the American otherness is characterized by his lack of integration, since people often discriminated against him. From an epistemological point of view, Cournos's experience is based on his need to have good knowledge of the people who surround him in order to adapt to the context as well as possible. Such knowledge, which increased as the years went by and his journey across the countries progressed, was useful to forge his personality and settle into a new culture. Although Cournos travelled many times from Europe to the USA, he did not fully adapt to the new surroundings and his book expresses his constant search for a land of his own, which he partly found in America.

3. Space-time coordinates in Nabokov's *Speak, Memory*

Nabokov employs a particular narrative approach in *Speak, Memory*, as the book is mostly "set" in the writer's solipsistic dimension and the events are not arranged in chronological order. The geographical places that he mentions in the text and the numerous references to childhood memories implicitly express the author's nostalgia for his past. Such nostalgia increases throughout the autobiography, as the writer conjures up different moments in his life until he explicitly compares the loss of his country to the loss of a part of himself:

> The break in my own destiny affords me in retrospect a syncopal kick that I would not have missed for worlds. Ever since that exchange of letters with Tamara, homesickness has been with me a sensuous and particular matter. [...] but give me anything or any continent resembling the St. Petersburg countryside and my heart melts. What it would be actually to see again my former surroundings, I can hardly imagine. Sometimes I fancy myself revisiting them with a false passport, under an assumed name. It could be done (250).

Nostalgia, as I have explained, has different overtones which marked Nabokov's experience. His nostalgia can be considered restorative, as he tries to "recompose" the world he misses, but the only way he has to return to that world is its evocation, the long imaginary journey in time that takes him to the Russian countryside. Nabokov's nostalgia is, however, also reflective, since it employs the powers of his imagination to travel back in time. The writer's effort to evoke his past is emphasized by the use of verbs of perception. In the passage quoted above, he uses such verbs as "see" and "fancy," which turn the time dimension into a visual one. The images of his past are portrayed through the eyes of his memory, and the past itself is recalled in the form of photographs[48]. In this regard, he traces back his strong link with the past to his mother. In the second chapter, he writes:

> To love with all one's soul and leave the rest to fate, was the simple rule she heeded. [...] She cherished her own past with the same retrospective fervor that I now do her image and my past. Thus, in a way, I inherited an exquisite simulacrum – the beauty of intangible property, unreal estate – and this proved a splendid training for the endurance of later losses. Her special tags and imprints became as dear and as sacred to me as they were to her (40).

Nabokov inherited from his mother the habit of looking at his past by means of "visions" and pictures. Such an ekphrastic mechanism, which takes him back in time through a succession of images, is connected with Bergson's concept of time. Nabokov draws inspiration from Bergson to express his reflective nostalgia, as he superimposes past images that are suddenly introduced into the present dimension of narration (Lyaskovets 2014, 2–3). This is the only way he has to dwell on the loss of his past: returning again and again to his country by recalling his memories and the main moments of his childhood. Owing to the use of analeptic and proleptic devices, the autobiography results in a constant "interaction" among past, present and future images. Time becomes reversible and can be manipulated by human imagination. In this steady interaction among the different axes of time, the author's subject, his consciousness, his "spiritual" entity, overshadow his self, his physical entity.

Nostalgia is thus connected with the nature of the author's itinerary. Nabokov's route in *Speak, Memory* is mainly imaginary and, as such, is described through the reflective nostalgia and the superimposed memories of the past. When he thinks about the years he spent in Cambridge, he writes: "And I thought of all I had missed in my country, of the things I would not have omitted to note and treasure, had I suspected before that my life was to veer in such a violent way" (261). Berberova, as I will explain, illustrates an "earthly" itinerary, because, unlike Nabokov's, it is not imaginary; it is a geographical, a real itinerary. As a consequence, her nostalgia is mostly restorative, since she tends to recompose her world by living in the Russian communities of Berlin and Paris. Cournos's

---

48 Lyaskovets (2014, 2–3) explains that "As a result of this visual thinking, Nabokov's texts create a narrative paradigm that evokes the temporal through an ocular appeal. Nabokov's narratives translate the temporal into the visual and by doing so they make this temporal perceptible and, for this reason, more understandable. In *Speak, Memory* it is photography and visual technologies which lend a spatial form to Nabokov's representation of time."

case is different, because, in spite of the "materiality" of his itinerary, since the writer often dwells on the places where he lived, he is deprived of his original world, owing to the fact that he emigrated at an early age, and is denied the possibility of restoring his childhood world in the lands of emigration. He expresses, therefore, his reflective nostalgia, as the only means he is left with to recall his distant place of birth. Nabokov, like any other émigré, follows the "rule" of the geographical dislocation and his nostalgia is conditioned by the imaginary nature of his itinerary. He retraces his journey by means of his consciousness and reflective nostalgia, whereas Cournos is an exception and expresses his reflective nostalgia (connected, therefore, with an imaginary route), in spite of the "materiality" of his itinerary.

Nabokov's itinerary was particular. Cournos's, Berberova's and Shteyngart's routes were characterized by their temporary *nóstos*, in its different characteristics, while Nabokov's *nóstos* was "partial," in that he returned to Europe, his second home, soon after his emigration from his country, but never went to Russia again. The other exile writers temporarily returned, for different reasons and in different circumstances, to their motherland. The return is usually preceded by feelings of excitement and great expectations, because the exile cherishes his or her memories and associates them with the places of his or her past. Their temporary return to their country increased, instead, their displacement and foreignness, with their consequent disappointment. Nabokov returned to Europe, his second country after his emigration from Russia. However, his *nóstos* is not represented by his return to Europe from overseas, as he does not include his years in the USA in his autobiography. As I have explained, *Speak, Memory* is entirely set between Russia and Western Europe. If we consider that Western Europe was his second home, we should wonder where exactly in Europe the writer returned. Although Nabokov lived only three years in Cambridge, he adapted to the new *milieu*. The "empathy" with the British city was not generated, however, by the restorative nostalgia, namely by the reconstruction of his homeland context. What made the writer feel at ease in the city was, instead, a third type of nostalgia, called nostalgia of the diasporic intimacy (Lolli, 2012/ 2013, 121–122), that is the exile's spontaneous adaptation to the host country, thanks to his knowledge of English, the first language he was taught as a child:

> [...] it was Cambridge that supplied not only the casual frame, but also the very colors and inner rhythms for my very special Russian thoughts. Environment, I suppose, does act upon a creature if there is, in that creature, already a certain responsive particle or strain (the English I had imbibed in my childhood). Of this I had my first inkling just before leaving Cambridge, during my last and saddest spring there, when I suddenly felt that something in me was as naturally in contact with my immediate surroundings as it was with my Russian past, and that this state of harmony had been reached at the very

moment that the careful reconstruction of my artificial but beautifully exact Russian world had been at last completed (269–270).

Nabokov sees Cambridge as his second home and, as such, his *nóstos* is actually a European *nóstos*, symbolized by his return to the city of adoption from another European city. The latter is not mentioned, but it could be assumed it was Paris, where Nabokov was living before his emigration to the USA. He claims that, after leaving Cambridge in 1922, he went back there after about seventeen years, around 1938–1939, the years that preceded his emigration overseas. The return to his second home, as happened to the other émigré writers, did not meet his expectations. Nabokov, who returned to Cambridge to look for an academic position, writes:

> [...] the visit was not a success. I had lunch with Nesbit at a little place, which ought to have been full of memories but which, owing to various changes, was not. [...] I tried to put myself into the same ecstatically reminiscent mood in regard to my student years as during those years I had experienced in regard to my boyhood, but all I could evoke were fragmentary little pictures: [...]. The dull day had dwindled to a pale yellow streak in the gray west [...] (272–273).

Cambridge presents a dull atmosphere and the writer cannot find consolation, in Wordsworthian terms, in the city. His reflective nostalgia, which ought to be reawakened by the English surroundings, turn out to be "unproductive" and leads but to oblivion, sadness and displacement. The *nóstos* is deceitful and does not return the same image of the same place as it used to be in the past.

Unlike Cournos, who often refers to unpleasant episodes in his work, Nabokov does not complain about the places of emigration. This was due to the fact that Cournos had to help his family to make ends meet at a very early age in America and tackled numerous problems, whereas Nabokov came from a well-to-do family. However, he does not avoid commenting on the conditions of his compatriots. After explaining the concept of the spiral, as a metaphor for his life as an emigrant, he dwells on the relationship between the Russian immigrants and the local people, that he calls "aborigines" (276):

> These aborigines were to the mind's eye as flat and transparent as figures cut out of cellophane, [...]. It seemed at times that we ignored them the way an arrogant or very stupid invader ignores a formless and faceless mass of natives; [...]. In Berlin and Paris, the two capitals of exile, Russians formed compact colonies, with a coefficient of culture that greatly surpassed the cultural mean of the necessarily more diluted foreign communities among which they were placed. Within those colonies they kept to themselves. Life in those settlements was so full and intense that these Russian *"intelligenti"* [...] had neither time nor reason to seek ties beyond their own circle (276–277).

The writer does not interact with the local people. His life took place within the circles of the immigrants, the real "promoters" of culture, according to him. Like

Berberova, as we will see, he lives in a "linguistic and cultural enclave," where communication with the local people was not frequent, although the social macrotext was to exert an influence over his background. I have claimed that Nabokov's nostalgia presents different overtones and that his experience included both reflective nostalgia and the nostalgia of the diasporic intimacy, as his route is mainly imaginary. However, the writer expresses his restorative nostalgia as well, which is related to the few "material," "earthly" moments of his path. He somehow reconstructs his life in the Russian "enclave" and "extends" the world of his native country to a foreign context. Nabokov, therefore, embodies all three types of nostalgia owing to the complex circumstances of his emigration.

As to the concept of "enclave," it is a linguistic-cultural space, included in a larger space, with a different language and culture. The enclave is a cultural area where émigrés can discuss and spread their ideas. It is the expression of the immigrants' "no man's land," which is strictly connected with the concepts of solitude and isolation. The latter can have a negative and a positive connotation, according to the context. Isolation usually evokes sadness and depression and has, therefore, a negative meaning (Klein 1984, 139–162), but, from another angle, it "sublimates" the émigré's experience and makes him or her aware of his or her condition of in-betweenness (Winnicott 2007, 29–39). The "no man's land" is a space of isolation, where people from a different cultural context gather and recreate their original world. From this perspective, it has a positive connotation, it is a place where immigrants share their condition and help each other.

The "no man's land" could be conceived as an imaginary space, unknown to alien people and to the world. As the "transplanted" place of the motherland, it stands for another example of heterotopia, that is another place, whose features are similar to the place it originates from. The heterotopic space that Nabokov creates is the ideal reproduction of Russia, where its inhabitants can share their common cultural background and are allowed, unlike at home, freedom of speech and thought. In its alterity, Nabokov's heterotopia is also a utopia, an ideal space which can exist outside the Russian borders only. The utopian traits of such spaces are emphasized by Nabokov himself when he writes: "I suppose it would be easy for a detached observer to poke fun at all those hardly palpable people who imitated in foreign cities a dead civilization, the remote, almost legendary, almost Sumerian mirages of St. Petersburg and Moscow, […]" (282). The writer refers to his homeland's culture as a non-existent civilization, which is artificially reproduced abroad, in the spaces of the "no man's land." The reproduction of an*other* civilization in a foreign country foreshadows the birth of transliterature. The borders of transliterature mark, however, the territory of real Russianness, as they delimit the space where the "authentic" Russian culture can spontaneously take root, without being "tampered" by the control of the Regime. Nabokov condemns those compatriots who comply with the rules of the Russian Regime and considers "[...] monstrously un-Russian and subhuman the behaviour of pampered authors in the Soviet Union, the servile response on the part of those authors to every shade of every governmental decree" (282).

Being part of the "no man's land" and, therefore, of the heterotopic space which is inhabited by the Russian intellectuals abroad, paradoxically means being a real Russian or, better, forming a Russian "subculture," "[...] alien to and isolated from the larger national culture (Brauner 2017, 2). Such a heterotopic space does not stand for a subculture of the Russian national culture; it is the truthful side of the source culture, devoid of the shadows of the Regime. The construction of the "no man's land" implies the immigrants' space-time dislocation. As such, it cannot exist without generating the exile's sense of displacement and his or her emigration to a place. The "no man's land" is not only the place of solitude, that is a state of isolation from the host country, and freedom, but also the place of the secret, where immigrants support those activities that are forbidden in their own country. It is both a tangible and an immaterial dimension, because it is formed in the immigrants' soul and becomes a private space, the only space where the exile can build his or her world. As such, the "no man's land," as the immigrant's private space, is a threat to the Regime; it includes the exile's expression of freedom as well as his or her private universe. It is a space of rebellion and, at the same time, a frontier, where immigrants spend an indefinite time of their life. As such, it can be regarded as a place of passage, of transience, where time and space merge. Living in that space means travelling in a spacecraft, where the lack of gravity subverts the space-time references, thus making it an a-temporal dimension[49].

From the spaces of the "no man's land," Nabokov takes the reader, in the final chapter, to the spaces of freedom that he recalls during his European years. Such spaces are identified with the numerous parks he visited in Berlin, Paris and Prague, as large areas where the writer is allowed to go along his imaginary itinerary. The European gardens and parks are so impressed in his mind, that they become travelling spaces. They seem to follow his route throughout Europe: "As time went on and the shadow of fool-made history vitiated even the exactitude of sundials, we moved more restlessly over Europe, and it seemed as if not we but those gardens and parks traveled along" (306). If the "no man's land" is comparable to a frontier, to a place where space and time lose their constraining aspect, the gardens and the parks become "joining" spaces, namely

---

49 In this regard, it is interesting to observe that Brodsky (1996, 155–156) compares his life to a spacecraft, which travels without reaching a specific destination. The spacecraft is the metaphor for the immigrant's life, whose itinerary includes different countries, like Russia and America, but, as he underlines, it dissolves the borders separating the countries and, therefore, space becomes a "continuum" of places. Likewise, he does not see, as an exile, any differences between the day and the night, but only a "continuum" of time.

areas that join the different lands the author crosses on his way to America. Nabokov often underscores their "movable" nature in the text, for instance, when he recalls the moments spent with his son in these parks: "The gardens and parks seemed to move ever faster as our child's legs grew longer, [...]" (307). Their motion follows, as seen, the author's journey. Unlike the "no man's land," where space and time are blurred, the gardens are space references along the writer's passage to the USA. They are places that, owing to their "movable" nature, provide him with the space-time coordinates of his voyage.

As occurs with the historical dimension of the text, which switches from the writer's subjective perspective, his private history, to the real one, that is to say the "public" history, the historical events that are hinted at in the authobiography, the author changes the perspective of his geographical route: he switches from his imaginary journeys to the real routes of his emigration. Towards the end of the text, Nabokov "returns" to his surrounding environment, the real world, and remembers the different steps of his exile in detail. After arriving in Crimea, he sets off with his family for Constantinople and Piraeus on board the *Nadezhda*, "Hope" in English (Boyd 1991, 11). As he starts his journey to Turkey and Greece, he compares the different stages of his "zigzagging" (251) voyage to the positions of the pawns on his chessboard. Once again, Nabokov recalls his past, his real "history" as an exile and retraces, with more geographical details, his itinerary throughout Western Europe before leaving for the USA. The thirteenth chapter starts as follows: "At the end of 1919, by way of the Crimea and Greece, a flock of Nabokovs – three families in fact – fled from Russia to Western Europe. It was arranged that my brother and I would go up to Cambridge" (253). As the end of the autobiography approaches, the author mentions his final destination and increases the reader's expectations, who might be curious to find out how his voyage ends. The geographical route that the author depicts in this section emphasizes even more the Nabokovs' plurilingual context. His parents stayed in London and then went to Berlin, and his brother Kirill attended schools in London, Berlin and Prague and spoke five languages. Nabokov's other brother, Sergey, taught English and Russian in Paris. The Nabokovs, therefore, were influenced by the European culture during their stay in the West. By interacting with the lively atmosphere of the European cities and, in particular, with the English-speaking context of Cambridge, Nabokov even "fears" the loss of his source language and is aware of the linguistic interferences brought about by the target culture. The writer himself states:

> My fear of losing or corrupting, through alien influence, the only thing I had salvaged from Russia – her language – became positively morbid and considerably more harassing than the fear I was to experience two decades later of my never being able to bring my English prose anywhere close to the level of my Russian. I used to sit up far into

the night, surrounded by an almost Quixotic accumulation of unwieldly volumes, and make polished and rather sterile Russian poems [...] (265-266).

In Cambridge Nabokov "sows" the first "seeds" of his English. Not only does he recognize "[...] the direct influence upon my Russian structures of various contemporaneous ('Georgian') English verse patterns that were running about my room and all over me like tame mice" (266), but he also starts his first translations into Russian of foreign works, like *Alice in Wonderland* and *Colas Breugnon*[50].

In the last chapter, Nabokov dwells on the descriptions of the gardens, as geographical backgrounds of his journey. The beauty of the gardens and their proximity to the sea let the reader visualize his final destination, which, however, the writer never reaches in the autobiography. The American continent is perceptible in the reader's imagination, it is presented as the writer's next "abode." The succeeding gardens of the past lead the reader along an imaginary route until, addressing his wife, Nabokov concludes his autobiography, as he is walking towards the liner and crossing the last garden at St. Nazaire's harbor: "There, one last little garden surrounded us, as you and I, and our child, [...], walked through it on our way to the docks, where, behind the buildings facing us, the liner *Champlain* was waiting to take us to New York" (309). The garden at the French harbor takes on an important meaning, since it encloses the geographical and the historical dimensions of the writer's itinerary. Nabokov stresses its "geometrical design" (309), which stands for the "earthly" mapping of his journey and, within the borders of this "blooming design" (309), he sees his past and present. The garden, in fact, "Laid out on the last limit of the past and on the verge of the present" (309), and foreruns the "transatlantic gardens" (309), namely the American lands and the beginning of a new route overseas. The last garden at St. Nazaire, therefore, is the border between Europe and America and comprises both Nabokov's three historical dimensions, his past, present and future, and his three geographical ones, Russia, Western Europe and America. The last garden intertwines Nabokov's historical and geographical dimensions, namely his diachronic and synchronic routes. The reader realizes that the autobiography contains some hints at the American world, some flashforwards or, better,

---

50 As regards Nabokov's linguistic "evolution," Roper (2015, 10) writes: "The flight to America, with the nightmare of war closing upon his wake, was the great stroke of luck – but, as with everything else, it had long been prepared for. The *real* mystery is how he contrived to be taught to read English at age four, before he read Russian; how he managed to have an American-style liberal constitutionalist for a father, who imbued him with Anglophilia and set him to dreaming about Anglophone lands. [...] Is it only in retrospect that he looks fully, if ironically, American? Or did he call a new America into being – a Lolitaesque, Nabokovian new land, layered with perplexities, rippling with edgy laughter – to ratify what he had known he would become?"

glimpses of the New Continent, but the writer never dwells on his American years. The close of the text emphasizes the writer's metaphorical route, stopping in France, with the funnel of the liner in the background, and leaves the reader with a sense of incompleteness.

The intertwinement of the historical and the geographical dimensions takes place, as suggested, by means of the various languages employed in the text. The chronotopic evocation occurs with the use of the languages of his past and present, in order to single out the different moments of his life and place them on a common linguistic level. The use of Russian, English and French responds to the writer's different needs to combine his past and present, before setting off on a new voyage overseas. At the same time, by overlapping the different linguistic codes, Nabokov fosters the dialogue among the cultural contexts he evokes, with the purpose of finding a common space where his plurilingual communication does not fade. He recreates a world, which is able to welcome his translingual identity (Scura 2008, 405). Drawing inspiration from an expression coined by Barthes, "Writing Degree Zero," I would like to conclude with a metaphorical comparison that could sound too imaginative or bizarre, but that exemplifies Nabokov's plurilingual approach. By evoking the mathematical procedure of the powers, the writer seems to 'raise' the foreign phrases and sentences to a common power, a common language (his target language), to the power of zero, in order to 'smooth' the linguistic disharmonies of his itinerary. Likewise, if any number which is raised to the power of zero always equals one, so every foreign sentence, be it written in French or Russian, if properly contextualised in its plurilingual narrative and 'raised' to a common language, will result in the same linguistic code. The writer's self-translation of the foreign phrases maintains the communication among his different linguistic worlds. Nabokov does not mean to lose the communicative effectiveness in the ambiguity of his universe, and the plurilingual writing is the only way to create an ideal homeland, different *personae* and space-time territories where, however, the heterogeneity of the world coincides with its homogeneity.

4. Berberova's autobiography and the Russian intelligentsia in Europe

Unlike Cournos, who often underlines the incidents of bullying in America and the effort he had to make to integrate into the target context, Berberova's *The Italics Are Mine* centers on the main Russian intellectuals she met in Western Europe. Her work contains frequent references to the Russian poets and writers she met and she explains the importance of being part of their community to integrate into the transplanted Russian context. Berberova "draws" an "enclave," namely a Russian island abroad, where her life is set. In particular, she writes about the immigrants' relationship with their new culture and claims that "Notwithstanding how many years a man had lived in the Western world, some were taking everything they could from this world, but others lived behind their own Chinese wall which separated them from it" (505). She recognizes that some émigrés easily settle in the host country, but others are not eager to integrate into their new environment and choose to live in their own cultural space, following their feeling of restorative nostalgia. Although the writer does not openly state her preference for her home or the place of emigration, as Cournos does, she implicitly expresses a "centripetal" attitude, namely her closeness to the Russian community and, therefore, to her origins. This does not mean that Berberova preserves a narrow-minded behaviour in the West, but it is clear, in-between the lines, that she proposes to forge her literary background in the immigrants' community of Europe. In particular, her approach is more "centripetal" in France, whereas in the USA she has a "centrifugal" approach, where she tries to establish good relationships with the Americans. Berberova stresses the cultural "imposition" that she perceives in France:

> France demanded submission more strongly, often changed people by force, 'fed' them whether they liked it or not – so that at times they even did not notice it. There were many reasons for this: there was the tradition of Russian Europeans who used to live in Paris; there was French literature, which had one way or another entered the consciousness of even the semi-intelligentsia in school years; émigré children growing up in France and bringing to their homes the ways of the new country; [...]. In America matters were completely different: there was no tradition of coming here; the pressure that existed in France to subordinate to French culture was non-existent; [...] émigré children [...] did not bring into their homes new ways of life (505).

The French epistemic universe, owing to historical reasons, exerted a remarkable influence on immigrants, but Berberova mainly interacts with the Russian community and means to avoid such an abrupt cultural impact. As to America, she is more enthusiastic about people: "And above all people. Yes, in my first years here there were not many more of them than on my last day in Paris. [...] the accessibility of people around became their primordial feature for me, their openness, their willingness to accept me [...]" (507). Her numerous journeys around the wide plains of the USA show that she was eager to explore an unknown, but charming, culture. Like Cournos, who repeatedly retraces his itinerary, Berberova travels along the borders of different spaces, each pertaining to a particular phase in her life. In the final chapter of her autobiography, she writes "I know I can return from my third stage to the second: take a ticket and for a time sail whence I came. I have done this twice. But a return to the first stage is impossible for me: I can return to Russia only along the tracks of this book" (521).

Her motherland has been left behind by now, and she only considers returning to West Europe, thus excluding Russia from her backward itinerary, whose space will be reached through the pages of her memories. Berberova loses her native dimension for good and looks for her identity in a foreign land. The past, according to Brodsky and to many other émigré writers, is the imaginary space of safety and can be reached with the strength of imagination. Her return to West Europe turns out to be disappointing, as when she returns to Paris she feels alone. She returns to an alienating place, where she does not find the familiar dimension generated by the effects of the restorative nostalgia.

The "no man's land" is an important concept in Berberova's experience as well, because it embodies her private space, her space of freedom, where she can build her private life and recreate the world she would have liked to see. The past "lies" in her memory and increases her nostalgia. Such nostalgia expresses the craving for an abstract dimension, for a space that does not exist anymore; it exists in the idyllic memories that the writer cherishes. Berberova expresses her restorative nostalgia and means to reconstruct her cultural background in a foreign land, living amid her compatriots[51]. As a consequence of this cultural reconstruction around her, she expresses the third type of nostalgia, the nostalgia of the diasporic intimacy, which enables her to adapt to her current environment, so that she can feel at home abroad (Lolli 2012/2013, 121). Restorative nostalgia, however, precedes the nostalgia of the diasporic intimacy, in that it "composes" the pieces that symbolize her native country. By recreating the motherland abroad, the exile is allowed to recreate her own world and adapt to her surroundings.

An attentive comparison between *Autobiography* and *The Italics Are Mine* reveals that the former portrays an "osmotic" relationship between its author and his environment, in that, living most of his existence abroad, Cournos had to interact with the local people in the English-speaking countries he crossed during his journey. The latter, instead, describes the Russian community in Western Europe, as Berberova lives among her compatriots abroad. From a sociological point of view, Berberova is less concerned than Cournos, Nabokov and Shteyngart with her relationships with the local people abroad, as she mainly interacts with the people of the Russian community. Her text, therefore, unfolds a Russian-speaking context within an English-speaking macrotext, characterized by a limited exchange of linguistic elements. Following Lotman's cultural model about the representation of two different cultures, in which the Russian world is

---

51 Most of the Russian intelligentsia emigrated to Berlin, which was the first West "mooring" owing to its geographical position. As a consequence of the repressive policy of the Russian Regime, the Russians created in the German capital a community, where they organized literary debates, read, wrote and published articles (Scura 2008, 395).

the inner circle and America stands for the outer one, it appears that the exchange between the two cultural spaces is more limited at the beginning of her emigration, in France, and increases when Berberova goes to the USA, where she integrates *de facto* into a foreign context[52]. The increased exchange between the inner and the outer dimension stands out when Berberova describes, as I have underlined, her journeys throughout the American lands. In this complex interaction between the writer's inner world and her environment, between the inner world and the physical spaces of emigration, Berberova discloses some metatextual thoughts about the meaning of the autobiography, whose aim is to "seam," to use her main metaphor, her inner and outer spaces. As to the composition of autobiographical works, she writes as follows:

> The first trait of modern autobiographies is the revelation of the self. The second: man often pretends to be not smarter, kinder, nicer, better, cleverer than he is, but worse, nastier, more stupid, and simple. Bely in his recollections sometimes took on the pose of an 'idiot' [...]. From which comes the device of writing the opposite of what is. Epicurus said: Hide your life. William Blake said: What can be understood by a fool does not interest me. From which comes the deliberate complication by authors or writings about themselves. [...] All this I must take into consideration when I decide at some point to write a book about myself (437).

As regards the issue of the author's reliability, Berberova writes that, "[...] when I decide to write about myself, all my masks will be stripped off and I will not have to pretend to be better or worse than I am" (438). In spite of her short digression, Berberova's autobiography is mostly linear and objective. Unlike Nabokov who, as I have pointed out, splits his personality into his "physical" self and consciousness, Berberova describes, like Cournos, the progress of her route and, at the same time, sometimes digresses from her "earthly" dimension to express some reflections on her life as an émigré. From Berberova's perspective, writing about herself means including her *self*, to recall the principle of the self and the subject, into the space of interaction with her compatriots, and employing her *subject*, the abstract dimension of her consciousness, to make her observations on her life as an émigré. Unlike Nabokov, however, who separates self and subject, as his work mostly lingers on his thoughts, Berberova does not separate them. As explained, her autobiography is mostly descriptive and retraces, like Cournos's work, the itinerary from East to West and back to Europe; it merges her occasional thoughts with the geographical spaces she often refers to.

---

52 In his semiotic model, Lotman uses two concentric circles to represent the relationship between the source culture, called IN, that is the cultural system the exile is familiar with and which is included in the inner circle, and the culture of the target language, called ES, that is the foreign cultural system, included in the outer circle (1975, 155–168).

In this analysis of autobiographies, we cannot leave out of consideration Berberova's different "condition," that is the "condition" of being a woman writer. While Ayn Randt, another Russian-American émigré of her time, stood out in the literature of emigration and implicitly asserted her *égalité* with men, Berberova dwells on her being a woman and its implications on writing. She writes: "I must – when I write about myself at some point – say that I never suffered from being born a woman. I somehow compensated for this *deficiency*, which I never felt as a deficiency" (438). She becomes aware of her identity by crossing different places. At the beginning of her autobiography, she seems as if she were ashamed of being a woman, but then claims that " 'femininity' was my asset" (438). Womanness is an ambivalent condition in that it means weakness and inferiority but, at the same time, symbolizes the strength to face the sacrifices that emigration entails. Owing to the contradictory concept of womanness, Berberova integrates her feminine side with her masculine side, the latter epitomized by her "physical and emotional endurance" (438). The writer recognizes her identity and is proud of the trials and tribulations she had to go through[53]. Her identity was forged by different cultures and stood out in the American literary context.

5. Shteyngart: a modern immigrant's autobiography

Nostalgia, integration, displacement, loss, unhousedness are some of the problems that émigrés mostly deal with, as discussed before. Shteyngart was not an exception in this regard, but obviously faced his problems in a more recent context. The writer's displacement starts at home, in Saint Petersburg, with the oppressive atmosphere of the Soviet Regime. Unlike Cournos, Nabokov and Berberova, who left their country years before the Cold War, in a different historical and political context, Shteyngart recalls his Russian years by mentioning the visible effects of the Communist Regime. His "visions" of Russia, in fact, are interspersed with the majestic monuments of the Regime. The memories of his autobiographical account, therefore, are tinged with the imposing symbols of the Communist propaganda. When he arrives in the New World, he deals with numerous problems, such as discrimination. He displays his frustration when he writes about his first days at school, where the people around him do not hide their "cultural disagreement." As he writes about his teachers, "They tell me to get rid of the great furry overcoat. Trim my unkempt, bushy hair a little. Stop talking to myself in Russian. Be more, you know, *normal*" (105). The first concept

---

53 Fraser (1996, 22) claims that Berberova "[...] has a warrior's will. [...] the trials endured by people like Nina are almost unimaginable."

he learns from the adults is *normality*, whose sociological overtones exert a strong influence over his socio-cultural background. As a boy, he strains to understand what normality is in the American context. Normality means being less awkward, more in compliance with the local fashion and, obviously, more self-confident. In addition, Shteyngart gives a bad portrait of African Americans: "Still, everyone knows what to do when you encounter a dark-skinned person: You run. Because they want to rape us very badly, [...] if they see a seven-year-old Russian boy walking down the street with his asthma inhaler, they'll come over and cut him to death" (110).

His origins hinder his socio-cultural integration: "They hate me because I come from the country our new president will soon declare to be the 'Evil Empire,' giving rise to the endless category of movies beginning with the word 'Red' – *Red Dawn, Red Gerbil, Red Hamster.* "Commie!" they shout, [...]. "Russki!" (119). The social problems he deals with in the USA increase the nostalgia for his country, in particular his reflective nostalgia, since his mother tongue is the only means he is left with to communicate with his native country[54]. The expression of his nostalgia is the evocation of the past, not only as the image of a time dimension, beside the present and the future, but also as the mighty expression of a godlike entity, which constantly hovers over the Shteyngarts: "The past is haunting us. In Queens, in Manhattan, it is shadowing us, punching us in the stomach. I am small, and my father is big. But the Past – it is the biggest" (32). The past, whose first letter is capitalized, contains the image of Russia, is part of his native country he will never do without. As a consequence of this close relationship with his motherland, Shteyngart's Russian identity overshadows his Jewish one, as he is indirectly connected with the Jewish world through his parents. Such a "secondary" identity is somehow retrieved at the Jewish school. However, as he writes, he is often bullied by his Jewish schoolmates: "*But I got cut down there for you!* [...] *I left Latin Lenin in Moscow Square just to get this circumcision.*" (119). The school restores his "second" identity, an identity his parents imposed on him. The circumcision marks his passage to a culture he is descendant of but, apart from that, he does not seem to be particularly keen on Jewish culture. The restorative nostalgia of the Jewish world is not authentic and he does not adapt to his new surroundings.

The writer's itinerary, however, becomes a journey in which his nostalgia gradually fades out and turns into a process of integration into what he used to see as an alien world. As the years go by, Shteyngart settles in New York and takes part in numerous parties. Unlike other émigré writers, such as Berberova, who

---

[54] Grinberg (2014, 70) defines Shteyngart's case "[...] an interesting hodgepodge – Russian pride and Soviet nostalgia coming from a man whose family fled the institutional Jew-hatred of a totalitarian regime."

mostly spent her life abroad among the people who shared her condition, he meets many American people and later integrates into American culture; his passage from his country of birth to the New World is the passage from his Russianness, "tinged" with Jewish traits, to his Americanness. However, his Jewish identity emerges overseas, when he attends the Jewish school and experiences the first contrasts with his mates, while his Americanness stands out during his temporary *nóstos*, when he returns to Russia and realizes that his Russian is not as fluent as it used to be before his emigration. Shteyngart's passage from East to West is characterized by different stages, and the succession of such stages creates his private space, his "no man's land," an imaginary space, where the immigrant can forge his own identity. Unlike Berberova, Shteyngart does not preserve, within the borders of this space, the subculture of his motherland, as a heterotopic dimension of another place. His private space is influenced by a new socio-cultural setting. It includes the outer elements of the contexts he goes through and arranges them by means of the cultural filters of his native country[55].

During his passage from Russia to America, Shteyngart sees different places, like Germany, Austria and Italy. He looks at the Western world from a Russian perspective and everything he sees in the West goes through the lenses of his source culture. He is astonished at the wealthy life he sees in Vienna and at the "colorful" atmosphere of the Italian landscape. His "no man's land" is crossed by different cultural signs, which generate a never-ending process of interlingual and intersemiotic translation: their specific meanings do not lie in each particular sign that Shteyngart's semiospheric dimension assimilates, but are gradually "composed" as these signs are translated and re-translated in the passage from Europe to America (Marrone 2018, 50). The solipsistic world of his "no man's land" is characterized by the fast evolution and the dynamism of his transcultural background. At the same time, however, another process occurs in Shteyngart's dynamic semiosphere. Since it is filled with different cultural elements and signs, his semiospheric space generates a movement of interaction among the elements themselves, but the saturation of the space gradually reduces such dynamism until it comes to a halt. The arrival in the USA marks this saturation and causes the writer's personal dimension to deal with the lack of space; it becomes a place where all "earthly" references are lost by means of a psychological process, which contrasts the dynamism of his cultural semiosphere.

---

55 Following Lotman's theories, Nöth (2006, 260) claims that "[...] the self-construction of a semiosphere does not only extend to the construction of its own boundary, but also to the 'chaos' which surrounds it, a chaos which makes the own internal structure appear the more orderly."

The writer's inner dimension undergoes a sudden change once he settles in the USA. The shock generated by the interaction with American culture "freezes" the dynamism of his semiosphere. It stops the time dimension, as the writer's reaction to his problems in the USA is silence. He cannot understand the new culture and, like a child who needs to analyze, study and listen to the surrounding environment before using the language, the writer withdraws into silence. As Shteyngart claims, "And within that silence, time itself has stopped. Within that silence, the words hang in the air, fluttering in Cyrillic, not entirely painless but without the power to bring back the small, unquestioning child at their mercy" (321). The "fluttering" Russian words cannot "soothe" the young Shteyngart, who is inevitably conditioned by the new American context and has a more critical view of the world. His mother tongue is to be overshadowed by the target language owing to the effect of language attrition, and silence is the writer's reaction against his alienating environment. Emigration implies a psychological trauma, as well as the writer's need for a therapy. And in fact, silence is also his reaction against his father's disagreement about his choice to see a psychoanalyst: "It would have been better if you had told me you were a homosexual," my father said when I told him I had started psychoanalysis. [...] mental hospitals were used by the Soviet state against its dissidents – there is another fear" (321). Silence is the expression of Shteyngart's subject, his consciousness, it takes him to his reflective dimension. Unlike the dissidents in his country, who used to be silenced by the Soviet Regime, Shteyngart's silence is generated by his choice to react against an alienating context.

Although *Little Failure* is the "product" of a journey that the author repeated after Cournos, Nabokov and Berberova, it presents some differences as compared with the autobiographies of the three previous émigrés. Such differences mainly derive from Shteyngart's personal experience and his different relationship with Americanness. Unlike his previous "colleagues," he was educated in the American schools and colleges, and those were the places where he could forge his American identity. Cournos attended some educational institutions in America as well, but was mainly forced to work, before deciding to move to England. Nabokov and Berberova were adult enough when they moved to the USA and mainly interacted with the Russian émigrés they met abroad. Shteyngart "develops" his Americanness in his teens and his insightful depictions of American life underscore the social issues of the West, like drug addiction, prostitution and the alienation brought about by progress and technology (the latter had already been denounced by Cournos). Shteyngart, therefore, offers a more truthful description of American life, as he does not dwell on his relationships with the literary communities of émigrés, as Nabokov and Berberova do. He analyzes the American context from a sociological perspective, focusing on his relationships with the local people, especially in the educational institutions he attended. In addition, he mentions the main American symbols that act as a background to his narration, like the McDonald's, the skyscrapers, the manipulation caused by advertising and the parks.

Little Failure, with its idioms and everyday language, reads like an ordinary autobiographical account and lacks Nabokov's "philosophical" digressions; however, it gives interesting insights into modern American life. Shteyngart takes the liberty of portraying the American sociological context as if he were a born and bred American and, even though he never loses contact with Russians, he unveils his Americanness in his autobiography[56]. Such Americanness stands out in his approach to language. Cournos and Shteyngart employ an "earthly" language which is associated with "material" aspects and the geographical spaces of their routes, but they still differ in the "earthliness" of their language. Cournos, as seen, makes use of a simple and clear language, typical of a newly English-speaking émigré, whereas Shteyngart goes beyond the borders of grammar and form, introducing different idiomatic expressions and even swear-words. Shteyngart's America is pictured by employing the typical local language and penetrating the main sociological aspects. As a result of his educational years in the USA, Shteyngart presents every aspect of American culture.

Another aspect of the writer's emigration is worth being re-discussed. Like many of the Russian émigrés, Shteyngart had to cross many European nations on his way to America, like Italy, a place that Cournos, Berberova and other artists, like Brodsky, visited during their passage to the West[57]. It could be assumed that Italy did not exert an important influence on such writers' transcultural background, because they did not learn Italian. Shteyngart gives an account of his itinerary and his stays in different European countries and, although he does not mention the reason why his journey included such countries, he clearly likes Italy, mainly for its art and colors. In his comparison between his country and Italy, Shteyngart makes fun of the Soviet souvenirs Italians were so keen to buy. He wonders: "Why Italians would want to buy such artifacts is now beyond me" (88). When the writer is in Italy, he links the Russian souvenirs to the past. Italy is a space of in-betweenness, a space which marks the passage between the past and the future. He is getting ready to leave Europe and to explore a new world. Russia

---

56 In an interview, Shteyngart says: "I think you sometimes get it from both sides, with native-born Americans asking if you're familiar enough to write about this country, and immigrants asking whether or not you're immigrant enough to be speaking to the culture of your parents, and what it's like to be displaced from that. I think, for me, I don't believe in these questions of authenticity. I think if you're a 1.5 generation immigrant, then you write about that life. If you're third-generation, then you speak to that experience" (Farwell, 2018).
57 Italy was to Brodsky a third space, the final destination of his journey from Russia to America. Although he died in the USA, he was later buried in Venice, which represents Brodsky's last space of emigration, placed between Russia and America, but closer to his native country. As to Brodsky's relationship with Italy, see Russo 2015, 125–158.

is part of the writer's historical dimension. If his experience is pervaded by strong solipsism, silence and his reflective nostalgia for his country, which embodies the diachronic route of his emigration, his itinerary and the geographical areas included in it illustrate the synchronic elements of his trip. The writer merges history with geography, his past with his present time, the vertical dimension of time with the horizontal dimension of his route. In particular, he frequently refers to the different places that he crossed and where he lived and, therefore, he mostly illustrates the geographical dimension of his long journey.

His return to the historical "setting" is represented by his visit to Russia in the final section, his temporary *nóstos* which, as occurred with the previous artists, resulted in a great disappointment. Being a contemporary writer, Shteyngart's emigration was characterized by a different "kind" of *nóstos*. Cournos and Berberova, for example, returned to their country for a short time and never went back there again, whereas Shteyngart has been back to Russia more than once[58]. When he tells about his return to Russia in 2011, he is aware of his linguistic displacement and the remarkable differences between his motherland and his adopted country, a paradigmatic comparison between the old and the new.

---

58 Grinberg (2014, 70) writes that "*Little Failure* is a balancing act. On the one hand, it hilariously and poignantly tells Shteyngart's story of leaving (and never quite leaving) Russia and coming to terms with America – from the early childhood in Leningrad, to his 'torturous' Jewish education in New York, to the secular public halls of the glorious Stuyvesant High School, to the pot-smelling dorms of Oberlin College. On the other hand, he attempts to generalize from his experience and create a paradigmatic ethnic identity story for the Russian-Jewish immigrant."

Chapter Three: Spaces of plurilingual interdialogism

1. The navigation of soundscapes in Cournos's autobiography

Although Nabokov is believed to have been the forerunner of the emigration of the Russian intelligentsia and, therefore, of transnational studies, Cournos deserves a remarkable position in this regard (Bozovic 2018, 180)[59]. The first elements of his transnational experience stand out in *Autobiography*, which encompasses different socio-cultural areas in Russia, the USA and Europe. In spite of his limited fame, he wrote a number of novels and stories, mostly about exile, but his autobiography is one of the earliest examples of translingual narrative, as a consequence of his emigration overseas on the eve of the twentieth century, which paved the way for the emigration of later Russian-born intellectuals. Set against the autobiographical writings by the translingual artists I have previously analyzed, *Autobiography* is characterized by its linearity, as well as by the clarity of its language. Although it might read like a "reportage" or a "travelogue" and seems to lack the fictional aspect of *Speak Memory*, it lends itself to a range of metalinguistic interpretations[60].

In light of Cournos's and Nabokov's biographical facts, one might wonder the extent to which their bilingualism or plurilingualism can be analyzed from the same perspective. Unlike Nabokov, Cournos might not have been proficient in different languages owing to his emigration, as seen, at a very early age, and thus he could not use Russian as a literary language. More than a bilingual or plurilingual writer, Cournos should be viewed as a translingual writer, owing to his

---

59 Trousdale (2011, 7) confirms "[...] Nabokov's central place in an emerging transnational canon", because he "[...] provides both a model and a point of reference" and is "[...] an ancestor in an affiliative intellectual family." Transnationalism has traditionally been regarded as "[...] the process by which immigrants build social fields that link together their country of origin and their country of settlement" (Basch, Blanc-Szanton, Glick Schiller 1992, 1).
60 de la Durantaye (2014, 165) emphasizes the fictional aspect of *Speak Memory*, as "[...] it does not tell a classical story. [...] it departs from the traditional forms autobiographies have taken."

"natural" choice to write his works in a non-native tongue (Apter 2006, 99). In his autobiography, he has a good memory of his childhood and recalls his family events from the age of four. His translingual background dates back to his stepfather, since "He knew Russian, German and Hebrew perfectly, and was a distinguished scholar to the last" (16). In addition, he writes about his first bilingual experience in the opening of his book, when he describes his German tutor:

> But I loathed German, and I recall with loathing the hours I spent, or rather wasted, in studying this tongue. German and I were probably incompatible, [...] my German lessons did not progress as well as they should, considering the number of hours I spent on them. [...] My text-book, like all books of its kind, comprised vocabularies and translation exercises: German into Russian, and Russian into German (25).

Cournos uses Hebrew words in the first part of the text, like "*kosher*" and "*shegetz* (A gentile boy)," (28–29) which he hears from his family and tutors, along with Russian words, such as "*byess* (devil)" and "*golubtchik* – darling" (34), and others, mostly referring to religion, like "*bogomoltzi* – pilgrims – [...] *radi Boga* – for God's sake," (13). In addition, the author dwells on his linguistic education as a child:

> And I went on with my Russian, my German and also with my Hebrew. I loved Russian poetry, and was early acquainted with the simpler lyrics of Pushkin, Lermontov and Nekrassov. I read Grimm's and Andresen's fairy tales in translation; also *Robinson Crusoe*; and the fables of Krylov and Lafontaine. I learned several chapters of Isaiah by heart. [...] I was too young to understand the significance of the words, but the sound captivated, as the sound of English was to captivate me later, as one is captivated by an infusion of a rich red wine. I had various tutors in Hebrew. [...] By then, I had my fill of those charming Ukrainian songs (40).

Cournos is "sensitive" to foreign sounds and often reads foreign books. Cournos's semiosphere is a great system, where texts, languages and signs interact among one another and whose boundaries clash and produce foreign signs. Such "frontier filters" mediate the communication between the writer's semiosphere and the new linguistic elements, thus creating new linguistic entities. The latter, however, do not evolve into complex linguistic systems. What characterizes Cournos's translingual writing is the employment of simple structures. *Autobiography*, as well as Cournos's literary production, can be considered a real example of translingualism, that is to say, of that semiospheric dimension in which the clash of different semiotic and cultural elements foreshadows a new linguistic dimension, namely the target language. The author writes within well-defined linguistic spaces and does not go beyond the complexity of foreign structures. The text might be quite comprehensible to any non-native English speaker and reads like a work written for an immigrant audience. Since Cournos emigrated at an early age and returned to his native country later in his life, we might suppose that he lacked the linguistic means to write in Russian. At the same time, his command of English might not have been as natural as a native speaker.

Cournos's plurilingualism is strictly connected with his transnational experience, which he describes in the fifteenth chapter, titled "Go, West, Young Man!" In this section, the writer retraces his family's emigration from Ukraine to the USA. As he writes, "there was talk between her [Cournos's mother] and stepfather about going to America" (54). This part of the text shows the first frontier that the author crossed: "Farewell, Russia! Farewell! – and I turned my inward gaze westward, as toward a fabulous land of milk and honey, promised and about to be realized" (55). His seventeen-day journey takes him to Liverpool (across Germany) where he sets off for Philadelphia, the City of Brotherly Love. The arrival in the USA discloses a totally unknown world, whose contrast between the rich and the poor is emphasized by the apparent miscegenation. Such a socio-racial background leads the author to a plurilingual dimension, where words and phrases are "refracted" and "decomposed" into manifold meanings, where every single word that he hears is analyzed in its possible multi-layered semantic facets. Although the comparison among different languages (English, Russian and Hebrew) is quite frequent (yet not as frequent as in *Speak, Memory*), the section about Cournos's passage to America depicts the plurilingual interdialogism among the author's three languages. It even dwells on the different overtones of the English expressions generated by the writer's interaction with a new linguistic context. Hebrew and Russian phrases, accordingly, often appear in the text, as the author attempts a contrastive analysis of the multi-layered meanings of the American English lexis (Wanner 2008, 669). The Russian and Hebrew words and phrases, as linguistic "fragments" from other cultures, seem to "semi-translate" the first unknown sounds and signs of American culture. They mark the writer's transition from the source language to the target language. Upon his arrival in Philadelphia, Cournos is bullied for his Jewish origins, not to mention the various episodes of harassment he has to put up with, due to the cultural clash he undergoes. His plurilingual awareness arises as he tries to dwell on the different sound overtones of the English words and phrases that he learns:

> My effort to accustom myself to English had its amusing side. A child learns to speak phonetically, and the language I heard about me did not predispose me to learn as I should. Thus it is that an immigrant learns to say, 'Gerrare here!' when 'Get out of here!' is meant; 'Whatzemarre wid you!' when 'What's the matter with you?' is intended. Many words I caught by ear had indeed no meaning at all to me, and I used them afterward with absurd, sometimes entertaining effects (70).

When he settles into the American context, Cournos analyzes the target language from an "intralingual" perspective, focusing on the sound effects of the words and their possible links with the most peculiar aspects of the environment. Even when he sells the "Pay-pers" (73), he seems to refer to his need for money, as proved by the adaptation of the word root to his "material needs." By reproducing the onomatopoeic aspect of the American English words, Cournos focuses on the dialogic dimension of the words themselves and tries to communicate with the context that he gradually discovers in the USA. The writer uses the "artistic" overtone of the phrases to understand his new plurilingual environment, where the onomatopoeic dimension of the language appears to be an effective means to have a more authentic dialogue with the American world. As Bakhtin (1979, 141) states, every word, in its pluridiscursive expression, conveys its social and cultural contextualization. The word, therefore, unearths the American speakers' idiolect and is the means that the immigrant uses to grasp the core of the linguistic setting. The border separating Cournos's source language from his adopted one emerges when his stepfather arrives in Philadelphia and, on seeing his newborn son, David, who was born in Philadelphia, exclaims "*Nastoyastchy Amerikanetz!,*" which means "a real American" (81). Cournos's stepfather recognizes the baby's American identity as a consequence of the linguistic and cultural passage.

In spite of the hardships of the writer's life as an immigrant which, as seen, lead him to compare his life to a "struggle for existence," he finds "consolation" reading English novels and translations of novels into English, like *The Three Musketeers*, *Around the World in Eighty Days* and *With Clive in India*. His readings, supported by an English speaking environment, provide him with the first linguistic tools to employ the target language in his works. He writes one of his first books, *The New Candide* (1924), in a state of happiness: "it is my happiest book, written in happiness, amidst my own chuckles" (93). He is confident that he will be able to settle into the new context, thanks to his newly acquired skill in English writing. Moreover, the linguistic tools that he assimilates in the New World allow him to make some comments on the American society and to question some typical stereotypes. He contrasts the urban American setting with the sylvan spaces of his native country; he even seems to miss his childhood places:

> Young as I was (or perhaps because I was young), ignorant as I was (or perhaps because I was ignorant), inexperienced and childlike as I was (or perhaps because I was inexperienced and childlike), I felt even then (felt rather than knew) the discrepancies of a social state that called itself civilized but was in reality a jungle in which crude human beings employed the coloration of noble ideas and ideals to cover up their predatory nature. This knowledge was intuitive in me, thanks to something in my heredity, and again to my upbringing, untutored and unspoiled, in the loneliness of the woods where, unbeknown to myself, I developed a simple vision, [...] The Russian woods, the mystical taint of my ancestors, were in me: they made the mirror which reflected what it saw.

Living mirror that it was and is, it longed to see and still longs to see *America* a *brotherly land dreamed of by prophets* and as yet unrealized anywhere (112–113, my italics).

In this passage, Cournos recognizes his bilingual condition and his privileged position as an immigrant, since he can compare his present and his past, the American society and the Russian woods, here seen as two contrasting phases of his life. The sylvan areas of his native country have made him similar to a *noble savage*, who is willing to preserve his unspoilt condition in the American society, which he compares to a "jungle."

Foreignisms are not frequent in the text, but Cournos's plurilingualism can be perceived. Thanks to his increased collaborations with publishing houses and journals in the USA, Cournos decided to depart for London on April 13, 1912 (the following day he learned about the sinking of the Titanic), where he expected to develop his literary career[61]. His transnational experience includes his visits, before arriving in London, to Paris, Naples, Rome and Florence, where his interest in Italian art and culture was revived. In spite of his long stay in the USA, he declares, once in London, that "I could not even speak English properly, as the English spoke it" (218). The different accent stands out and the writer soon expresses some comments on it, by trying to reproduce a few phrases that he hears around him. He quotes a sentence uttered by a man, who explained the reason why a woman had died: "[...] she got in the w-wye (way)! Just like a woman!" (216), during a demonstration staged by local men to claim their right to vote. In addition, he mentions a cockney expression that is being referred to his appearance: "I sa-ay, Bill, is it Bikon or is it Shikes-pirr?" (216).

The atmosphere in London soon appears lively, owing to the Shakespearean culture that he perceives. The British capital meets his expectations and the writer is impressed, as he claims, by its [...] polyphonic revelation" (218). Cournos tries to understand London's heterogeneous context by using an intralingual translation[62]. According to Jakobson (1959, 233), "Intralingual translation or *rewording* is an interpretation of verbal signs by means of other signs of the same language." Likewise, Cournos interacts between two English-speaking spaces in his passage from the USA to England. He tries to understand the different accents and overtones of English in the new British context by means of an endolinguistic translation. The interpretation of the different aspects of the language, i.e. the intonation, the vocabulary and the accent, allows Cournos to understand the

---

61 As Smith (2013, 76) states, notwithstanding "America became his [Cournos's] 'homeland' [...] he felt strongly the call of England as a literary homeland, homeland of the language and literature to which he aspired."
62 Jakobson (1959, 233), in his famous essay, singles out two other types of translation: "2) Interlingual translation or *translation proper*, is an interpretation of verbal signs by means of some other language. 3) Intersemiotic translation or *transmutation* is an interpretation of verbal signs by means of signs of nonverbal sign systems."

various aspects of two different cultures. The writer undergoes, therefore, both a cultural displacement, which involves his passage from America to England, and an "intralingual" displacement, characterized by a geographical dislocation across two same-language contexts, but with different linguistic peculiarities (Cronin 2000, 9–16). It is exactly at Hyde Park where Cournos hears the British accent and where, as he writes, "I first got the idea for writing my novel, *Babel*" (218), whose title conveys, as he goes on writing, "[…] the dis-unity of our time, that dis-unity which presaged the approaching catastrophe and crash of the Western civilization" (218). Accordingly, Cournos becomes fully aware, in this area of London, of his plurilingualism, and is somewhat puzzled by the effects of his linguistic experience. What seems to worry him is the delay with which he learns English. Cournos's linguistic hybridism is based on an elementary knowledge of Russian and Hebrew and on a more sophisticated command of English that, however, "discloses" too many foreign constructions to be considered his mother tongue. When in London, he decides to write a book in English about American art and comments on his writing efforts:

> I was able in those days, […] to construct long elaborate rhythmic sentences with a surer sense of grammatical adequacy than to employ properly the commonplaces of English fitted into the language by usage. In any event, it was not always a matter of correctness; a person relatively alien to English might construct a sentence grammatically correct yet be utterly wrong from the point of usage. 'One should write as one talks,' was Ford Madox Hueffer's way of putting it – actually, Henry James, whom Mr. Hueffer admired, talked as he wrote, strange as that may seem – but then does any one but an Englishman talk like an Englishman? (248)

After writing in English, Cournos makes further observations about the target language in *Autobiography*. He claims that English is "transient" and even quotes Conrad's attitude to English as a foreign writer:

> Actually, too, Mr Hueffer once said to me, English has no grammar; it is mostly a matter of usage. Joseph Conrad, he insisted, notwithstanding the super passages of his prose, violated the English language most abominably, but was a great writer in spite of it. Conrad, by the way, spoke English like a foreigner, with a decided accent. Yet seven years later, Clement Shorter, who had also met Conrad, was to tell me that he would not have been able to tell from my speech that I was not an Englishman (248).

Cournos knows that English is not easy at all, since its structures present a particular combination of words and phrases and often go beyond the "frontiers" of grammar. The "transient" character of the English language shows the writer's exilic condition who, in turn, becomes aware of the consequences of his linguistic "fragmentation." By writing *Babel* (1922), he means to underscore his "gaps" in the languages he speaks, Russian and English, namely the lack of linguistic unity that spurs him to constantly look for a fixed abode, along with a language that he can finally consider his *lingua mater*. *Babel* emphasizes Cournos's search for a language of his own, that language that his never-ending emigration prevented him from learning as a native speaker. Cournos returned to Russia in 1917, since he was officially invited by the British Foreign Office to join the Anglo-Russian Commission in Petrograd. His return to Russia increases his displacement. The return to his homeland might have restored him to his original identity, even for a few weeks; however, his future is foretold by a French fortune teller that he meets at an evening with some friends:

> 'I see a young man [...] a young man....I do not think you know him yet....He is traveling between two countries...back and forth...back and forth...No, you do not know him yet....In another year, perhaps....And he will take you to a distant country... in connection with some work. I cannot tell you what country it is.... But it is overseas....' (294)

The fortune teller's prediction depicts Cournos's real life, characterized by the steady emigration from one place to another. The return to Russia does not offer him any relief, and it soon turns out to be disappointing, due to the poverty he sees there[63]. He even witnesses the *coup d'état* by the Bolsheviks and returns to London, where his literary career is crowned by the publication of *The Mask* (1919) and *Babel*. Cournos spent his life in England until 1922 when, after the publication of *Babel*, he decided to return to the USA to visit his family; then, he went to London again to continue his literary life. As can be easily inferred, the writer was always on the move and, as a consequence of his restless life, his work is imbued with plurilingual and transcultural elements that gradually affect his American identity; he sometimes quotes passages from American and English poets, like Whitman and Coleridge.

The structural simplicity of *Autobiography* shows that the author's linguistic background was still *in fieri*. Although he does not often use foreignisms, unlike Nabokov, and, as the story progresses, the contrastive comparisons with other languages are less frequent, the work reads like an implicit translation from Russian into English. The author, in fact, "translates" his itinerary from his source language into his target language, but does not do so by employing the tools of the source language. He interacts with the target context by using its cultural signs and symbols. Indeed, Cournos's translation is not influenced by the linguistic environment of his mother tongue, but tends to recreate the world around him by employing the expressive and cultural tools of the target language.

---

63 As Ayers (2011, 357) writes, "Cournos did not stay long in Russia once the October Revolution had begun, claiming in his *Autobiography* that his stay there no longer had a purpose, and escaping via Murmansk in an adventure that is given more narrative space in that book than the Revolution itself."

Such a "dynamic" process absorbs voices from different cultures and creates a hybrid text, where cultural and linguistic expressions interact but, at the same time, do not complete one other, do not form a complete linguistic configuration in the writer's semiospheric system, due to the continuous exchange of linguistic and cultural elements generated by the writer's routes (Godayol 2002, 117). He writes in English as if he were translating his thoughts into the adopted language, describing the New World from a transcultural perspective. As a result, the reader perceives the writer's linguistic and geographical displacement, owing to the dynamic background of the autobiography, which dwells on different geographical areas, and to the fact that the linguistic structure of the text meets the foreign reader's needs.

The different semantic overtones of the lexis employed by the author do not conceal the sense of foreignness throughout the text. At times, the reader might have the impression that the author uses the Russian syntax with the English vocabulary, as if his native tongue were hidden below the surface of the English handwriting. Such foreignness seems to be preserved in order to make the book suitable for any immigrant, as well as to make the reader realize the writer's effort to adapt to the changes of the setting. Cournos tries to "uproot" any monolingual effects from the text, a process that Nabokov will emphasize, and to blur the fragile frontiers among his linguistic spaces (Bozovic 2018, 176).

The simple structures of the sentences and the vocabulary are the consequence of a linguistic loss and the lack of communication with his native country. Such simplicity can be explained by means of the theoretical approaches of "henolingualism," that is, a compromise between patriotism and cosmopolitanism, monolingualism and plurilingualism (Espino Barrera 2017, 193). In light of this, the book (and the other plurilingual autobiographies analyzed in this study) can be regarded as a "henolingual" work: despite its general linguistic "uniformity," the text comprises in itself the author's different linguistic identities. Being expressed in English, the author's identities are narrative spaces, which are "located" in-between the monolingual condition originated in the native country and the voices from different cultural contexts. And yet, such a definition might not be complete. If *Autobiography* can be firstly considered an attempt to implicitly self-translate Cournos's life from the Russian world into the American one, it could be added that, more than a self-translation, the work narrates his linguistic route, his passage from Russian to English. The linguistic "evolution" leads to the search for new semantic spaces, which replace and complete the writer's childhood linguistic education. For this reason, it might be wrong to regard Cournos as a bilingual writer, owing to the partial acquisition of his two childhood languages, Russian and Hebrew, and to the fact that English was his target language. The communication among his different consciences produces a constant dialogue, as well as more complex cultural clashes, with new linguistic experiments. At the end of the book, the author recognizes his translingual identity in America, which he praises for its cultural and social dynamism and where he partly finds his final abode: "America is an energy. And energy is good. In the past America has harnessed its energy for material power. [...] Niagara Falls is to me the physical and spiritual symbol of America. When America harnesses its spiritual energy as it has harnessed the Falls it will become a great country, a marvellous country" (344). In contrast to Nabokov, who finds his permanent residence in the "third space" of Switzerland and never returns to Russia, Cournos sees America as his home, notwithstanding its manifold contradictions[64].

2. Geographical and linguistic dislocations in Nabokov's *Speak, Memory*

Speak, Memory is one of the most enigmatic works written by Nabokov, owing to the manifold interpretations it lends itself to, along with the peculiar hybridism of its diegetic structure[65]. As critics have often underlined, the classical overtone of the title, which implores the writer's memory to disclose his past, does not meet the reader's expectations and reveals a completely different text, whose boundary between autobiography and fiction is sometimes difficult to detect (de la Durantaye 2014, 165; Boyd 2011, 270–271). By recalling his childhood, the author emphasizes, as criticism has often suggested, the traumatic experience of leaving his own country and, as a result, "[...] the poignant reminiscences of family history" (Ponomareff 2013, 405). The memories of his English, French and Russian tutors express, with different intensities, his nostalgia for his motherland. What is more, by "unearthing" his memories, he traces an imaginary vertical route, which leads the reader to his solipsistic world and shows the diachronic dimension of the text[66].

---

[64] In an interview to Nabokov, Appel (1967, 127) asked the following question: "For years bibliographers and literary journalists didn't know whether to group you under "Russian" or "American." Now that you're living in Switzerland there seems to be complete agreement that you're American. Do you find this kind of distinction at all important regarding your identity as a writer?" Nabokov's answer was: "The writer's art is his real passport. [...] I think of myself today as an American writer who has once been a Russian one." Smith (2013, 77–96) states that Cournos's passage from Europe to America is "[...] the passage from a homogeneous culture into the diverse and fragmented culture of the new homeland."
[65] Voronina (2016, liii) claims that "In *Speak, Memory*, Nabokov weaves patterns of the past into a 'magic carpet' that the reader can fold and unfold while traversing through the text."
[66] Boyd (1991, 521) claims that Appel's review of *Speak Memory* "[...] identified the aim of all his work as 'the transcendence of solipsism.'"

The historical configuration of the autobiography, which comprises its vertical dimension and unveils the author's past, intersects with the horizontal space of the text, characterized by the numerous geographical references. Although the autobiography starts, as I have said, with a programmatic statement, which outlines the historical and geographical setting of the narrator's work, the diegetic structure of the text mixes different space-time and cultural levels. The intersection of the historical and geographical dimensions questions the narratological structure of the text and its linguistic aspect. Along the borders of these two dimensions, the author's self plays an important role as a "mediator" among different languages. One of the most significant sentences in the text is emblematic in this regard: "I learned to read English before I could read Russian" (79). The writer often uses the pronoun "I" since his *ego* is the axis around which his two linguistic worlds revolve. Following Barthes's (2003, 26–27) theory, the different linguistic contexts that Nabokov constantly conjures up become more authentic, as he narrates the first forty years of his life by combining the use of the first-person singular pronoun with the past simple. The first-person singular pronoun conveys realism and is less fictional than the third-person singular pronoun, owing to the illusory atmosphere that the third-person singular pronoun tends to create. The past simple "grasps" and isolates past events in order to make them plausible, even when they originate from the writer's fictional world. It is the tense Nabokov uses to recall his childhood, his own memories and, by employing it with the first-person singular pronoun, he recollects his past events within the personal sphere of his own *ego*, emphasizing the truthfulness of his story. Unlike the third-person singular pronoun, which is usually used to depict an imaginary world, his *ego* is relocated from the fictional space to the real one, his past. As Barthes (2003, 26) claims, such pronouns as 'he,' 'she' and 'it' are actors, whereas the pronoun 'I' is the witness. Although criticism has often asserted that *Speak, Memory* presents a blurred boundary between autobiography and fiction, Nabokov resorts to the past simple and the first-person singular pronoun to redefine the borders of his plurilingual universe, as well as his relationship with the different cultural and linguistic contexts[67].

The use of "I" in the text, which actually mentions but a few historical events and focuses on the writer's personal history, preserves Nabokov's historical and linguistic background. Like Berberova, he can be considered "[...] an indefatigable collector and archivist of the self" and appears "[...] a powerful creator of himself" (Peterson 2001, 494). The "graphic perpendicularity" of the first-person singular pronoun typifies the vertical configuration of time and, therefore, the

---

67 Cooper (2016, 26) underlines that "[...] the experience of Bergsonian *durée* softens the boundaries between self and others, offering a route into a shared, inter-subjective consciousness."

writer's diachronic "axis" which "unearths" his memories. The pronoun contains in itself Nabokov's impenetrable history; it generates new linguistic frontiers by repeatedly intersecting with the horizontal geographical spaces of the text. It breaks contacts with the "public" dimension of the writer's history and "explores" his background.

Nabokov's memoirs portray a parallel world, pervaded by "[...] connecting links, [...], oblique resemblances, topsy-turvy mirrors" (Wellek and Warren 1956, 79). As Nabokov describes his childhood, he explores his inner dimension, which is gradually "contaminated" by plurilingual elements in different contexts. In the previous chapter, I have claimed that the heterotopic space is the imaginary space that the writer, from a sociological point of view, constructs to "retrieve" the memories of his motherland. From a linguistic angle, Nabokov's heterotopic space is created within the borders of a heterolinguistic space, where his plurilingual identity comes into being. In this imaginary, but constantly present space, different cultural and geographical places overlap. It is the "translated" world of a parallel life, where the writer imagines his existence as a speaker of a different language, be it Russian or French, but not English, his target language[68]. Nabokov's plurilingual identity is amplified by the ceaseless intersections of the synchronic and diachronic routes in *Speak, Memory*. French and Russian words and phrases are frequent among the intertwined memories. They "voice" the writer's bilingual and/or trilingual world and the "reconstruction" of his past amid the influence of different linguistic codes. His own world becomes his private history, with the account of numerous seemingly trivial events that are, however, important to the diegetic development of the text. Nabokov discloses his inner world by describing singular moments in his life and dwelling on their details (Appel 1967, 32)[69]. At the same time, the most important historical events of this period, like the war between Russia and Japan in 1904 and World War One, act as a background and are only hinted at. Some examples of the evocation of the writer's particular moments of his childhood could bring into focus the strict relationship between his solipsistic universe and the development of his plurilingual identity.

---

68 The constitution of a parallel world and, thus, of a heterotopic space, might be considered the author's attempt to conceive new expressive devices in a foreign language. As Boyd (1990, 292) claims, "The true story of Nabokov's art is the story of his finding the formal and fictional inventiveness to express all the problems his philosophy poses. By the end of the 1920s, he had not only rejected the second hand words and devices of his early poetry, he had also left behind the direct meditations of stories like 'Sounds,' 'Grace,' or 'A Guide to Berlin,' [...]. As his talent burgeoned he discovered new structures and strategies that would allow his ideas their full intellectual value *and* a human context that gave them a local habitation and a name."
69 As regards the nature of *Speak, Memory*, Nabokov (1990, 77) claims in an interview that "*Speak, Memory* is strictly autobiographic. There is nothing autobiographic in *Lolita*."

One of the earliest memories that Nabokov recalls to strengthen the ties between his past, his historical dimension, and the evolution of his geographical route in the present time of the narration, is a game he used to play behind a sofa at home at the age of four. He remembers when he used to separate the sofa from the wall in order to create a space behind it. Such a space formed a "narrow passage" (23) and he often "[…] had the fantastic pleasure of creeping through that pitch-dark tunnel" (23); then, he would "[…] reach the tunnel's far end, […] and be welcomed by a mesh of sunshine" (23). This is one of the first things he tells about his childhood and, although it might not sound relevant to the rest of the text, it is an unconscious act that foreshadows his future route as a plurilingual exile. By pretending to cross the narrow passage, he seems to foresee his geographical itinerary, the same crossing that would take him far away some years later. Reaching the end of this passage means fulfilling his dreams. As a result, one of the many memories that might have been written with the only purpose of romantically enjoying his past, becomes an emblematic image that would open new spatial and linguistic horizons in the writer's years to come. The passage foreruns his transnational route and stands for the heterotopic counter-space characterized by the overlapping of cultural and linguistic environments; it is the first expression of Nabokov's plurilingual identity.

The detailed account of his personal daily events presents, as explained before, the sudden inclusion in the work of some hints at certain historical events, like his father's arrest by the tsar and the outbreak of World War One. The historical memories, even those belonging to the "public" sphere, compose the writer's imaginary travel. Criticism has often focused on the "fragmented" structure of *Speak, Memory*, as well as on its timeless dimension and the lack of the chronological arrangement of the events. The steady historical and geographical dislocations illustrate his plurilingual and transnational identity (Cooper 2018, 39). The transnational elements are present throughout his memories and are mostly introduced by his tutors, nurses and relatives, who are always associated with precise historical and geographical references. Since Nabokov and his brother "[…] could read and write English but not Russian" (28), their education was entrusted, when still living in Russia, to their village schoolmaster, Vasiliy Martïnovich Zhernosekov. Another example lies in the third chapter, in which Nabokov mentions an English governess during his stay in Nice in 1903, when his mother was taking care of his sick grandfather, and describes some of his relatives who often travelled abroad, like his Uncle Konstantin, a diplomat. When he remembers the day he met Uncle Konstantin in London, Nabokov quotes one of the first significant sentences in Russian that his father uttered: "*Mï v Anglii, mï v Anglii* [we are in England]" (60). Such an exclamation includes a linguistic *mise an abyme*, namely the playful use of the languages, which combines foreign phrases and sentences, as mirrors of different linguistic identities[70]. The text is gradually imbued with foreignisms, which come into being by the intersection of the historical and geographical references. Another remarkable example of geographical dislocation in the text stands out when the narrator dwells on his Uncle Ruka, his mother's brother, who worked in the diplomatic service. The portrait of his uncle takes him along an imaginary journey across different places:

> After a brief stay in Rozhestveno he would go back to France or Italy, to his château (called Perpigna) near Pau, to his villa (called Tamarindo) near Rome, or to his beloved Egypt, from which he would send me picture postcards (palm trees and their reflections, sunsets, pharaohs with their hands on their knees) crossed by his thick scrawl (69).

As a result of his numerous journeys, Uncle Ruka often uses foreign expressions in his dialogues, to unveil his increasingly plurilingual and multicultural self. He is an emblematic "character" in the autobiography. The author emphasizes his gift for languages:

> He prided himself, however, on being an expert in decoding ciphered messages in any of the five languages he knew. We subjected him to a test one day, and in a twinkle he turned the sequence "5.13 24.11 13.16 9.13.5 5.13 24.11" into the opening words of a famous monologue in Shakespeare. [...] He sang barcaroles and modish lyrics ("*Ils se regardent tous deux, en se mangeant des yeux...*" "*Elle est morte en Février, pauvre Colinette!...*" "*Le soleil rayonnait encore, j'ai voulu revoir les grands bois...*" and dozens of others). He wrote music himself, of the sweet, rippling sort, and French verse, curiously scannable as English or Russian iambics, and marked by a princely disregard for the comforts of the mute *e*'s (70–71).

Uncle Ruka's talent is so remarkable, that he even sometimes uses French and Russian in his conversations with people:

> [...] his speech was a fastidious combination of French, English and Italian, all of which he spoke with vastly more ease than he did his native tongue. When he resorted to Russian, it was invariably to misuse or garble some extremely idiomatic or even folksy expression, as when he would say at table with a sudden sigh [...]: "*Je suis triste et seul comme une bylinka v pole* [as lonesome as a 'grass blade in the field']." (71)

Nabokov always translates into English the foreign expressions. The short evocations of the different geographical spaces, which intersect with the diachronic space of the text, originate transnational discourses as a result of the combination of foreign phrases. Among Nabokov's relatives, Uncle Ruka stands out as one of the "characters" who personifies the mixture of the historical and geographical coordinates. At the end of the third chapter, the writer remembers his Uncle Ruka, in 1908 or 1909, who used to read some French stories for children.

---

70 As regards Nabokov's narrative tricks, see Wyllie 2016, 1–19.

Nabokov is thrilled when he rediscovers, years later, those same stories, written by the Russian-French writer Mme de Ségur, as they remind him of his uncle. These stories actually anticipate Nabokov's transnational experience. He claims, in fact, that Mme de Ségur "[…] in writing them […] was Frenchifying the authentic surroundings of her Russian childhood which preceded mine by exactly one century" (76).

As Nabokov goes on recalling the various people who moulded his education as a child, he mentions different English nurses. He points out that he improved his English thanks to the help of such nurses as Miss Rachel, Miss Clayton, Miss Norcott, Miss Hunt, Miss Robinson: "A bewildering sequence of English nurses and governesses, […], come out to meet me as I re-enter my past" (86). The interaction with the English world shakes Nabokov's semiotic system. Russian, however, still played a major role in the writer's plurilingual world and was his main language. As he writes, "At a certain point they [Nabokov's English tutors] faded out of my life. French and Russian took over; and what little time remained for the speaking of English was devoted to occasional sessions with two gentlemen, Mr. Burness and Mr. Cummings" (87). By means of the foreign people he met, Nabokov illustrates his transnational itinerary, which is characterized by long moments of discontinuity between one language and another and, as a result, by an increased sense of displacement. The author partly attributes his plurilingual education to his father:

> The English and French governesses we had in our childhood were eventually assisted, and finally superseded, by Russian-speaking tutors, […]. In choosing our tutors, my father seems to have hit upon the ingenious idea of engaging each time a representative of another class or race, so as to expose us to all the winds that swept over the Russian Empire. I doubt that it was a completely deliberate scheme on his part, but in looking back I find the pattern curiously clear, and the images of those tutors appear within memory's luminous disc as so many magic-lantern projections (153–154).

A certain Mademoiselle, who arrived from Switzerland in the winter of 1905–1906 and stayed with Nabokov's family for seven years, personifies the writer's problems as an immigrant. Nabokov highlights Mademoiselle's limited Russian vocabulary, which

> […] consisted, […], of one short word, the same solitary word that years later she was to take back to Switzerland. This word, which in her pronunciation may be phonetically rendered as 'giddy-eh' (actually it is *gde* with *e* as in 'yet'), meant 'Where?' And that was a good deal. Uttered by her like the raucous cry of some lost bird, it accumulated such interrogatory force that it sufficed for all her needs (98).

Mademoiselle's steady repetition of "giddy-eh? giddy-eh?" sounds like the writer's search for a familiar context and expresses his linguistic problems. As Nabokov writes when he refers to the Swiss governess, the repetition of such question emphasizes her need "[...] to find out her whereabouts," "[...] to express supreme misery: the fact that she was a stranger, shipwrecked, penniless, ailing, in search of the blessed land where at last she would be understood" (98). Nabokov stresses the "metasemantic" overtone of Mademoiselle's "stock phrase," as it joins the gaps separating the linguistic phases of his transnational route. The Russian, English and French nurses and tutors played, as seen, an important role in Nabokov's plurilingual education. When Mademoiselle asks her question, she somehow conveys the author's need to settle into a new linguistic context. Hence, the phrase "giddy-eh?" semantically joins the languages Nabokov uses; it has a "metatranslational" function, which allows the writer to recompose the geographical and historical coordinates of his transnational experience, in order to adapt to the new surroundings. The Swiss woman's question stands for "[...] the pressure which Russian puts on Nabokov's Anglo-American" (Steiner 1970, 125), namely the writer's unconscious *ego* and its need for a familiar geographical and historical setting. It stresses his effort to communicate within his linguistic *mise en abyme* and to "join" the linguistic "fragments" associated with the different moments in his life[71]. A spatial element that reveals the Swiss governess's sense of displacement is also her room, which differs from the rest of Nabokov's house:

> Mademoiselle's room, both in the country and in town, was a weird place to me – a kind of hothouse sheltering a thick-leaved plant imbued with a heavy, enuretic odor. Although next to ours, when we were small, it did not seem to belong to our pleasant, well-aired home. In that sickening mist, [...], the lamp burned low, and strange objects glimmered upon the writing desk (107).

Mademoiselle becomes the author's "spokeswoman" from a linguistic and spatial perspective, owing to her sense of frustration and isolation. She "reconstructs" a space of her own inside Nabokov's family in order to preserve her cultural identity. Her room "reproduces" Switzerland's geographical space, where she keeps pictures of her family and country. Her diversity is thus emphasized by the peculiarity of her room and by her short dialogues, containing frequent French phrases, uttered in an unusual way. As the writer claims, she "[...] never found out how potent had been the even flow of her voice. The subsequent claims she put forward were quite different" (107). The French contamination of her dialogues stands out when she recalls some past moments with the Nabokovs: *"comme on s'aimait* – didn't we love each other! [...] *Ah, la fessée que je vous ai flanquée* – My, what a spanking I gave you!" (107). Mademoiselle's behaviour is

---

[71] As regards the device of the *mise en abyme* in *Speak, Memory*, it has been claimed that "[...] *Speak, Memory* embeds a mise en abyme that reveals the relationships between narrating author and remembered self in autobiography and Nabokov's other fictions, thus contributing to enhancing the halo of unreality of the whole" (Bontila 1999, 70).

an expression of the restorative nostalgia, which brings to light the diachronic dimension of the text. The governess's action is dictated by her will to reconstruct, to restore her lost abode and to return to her original place. As a result, she tries to reproduce her own world in an alienating space, with the purpose of overcoming her condition of unhousedness. Mademoiselle mirrors Nabokov's frustration as an exile and his search for his own identity (Mirabelli 2012, 7)[72]. Her influence on Nabokov is confirmed by the writer himself:

> And, really, her French was so lovely! [...] My father's library, not her limited lore, taught me to appreciate authentic poetry; nevertheless, something of her tongue's limpidity and luster has had a singularly bracing effect upon me, like those sparkling salts that are used to purify the blood. This is why it makes me so sad to imagine now the anguish Mademoiselle must have felt at seeing how lost, how little valued was the nightingale voice which came from her elephantine body (113–114).

Although Mademoiselle is not an exile, Nabokov "employs" her in order to express the immigrant's problems in a foreign context. Owing to the role she had in his family, the author keeps a good memory of her in the autobiography.

3. Plurilingualism and entomology

Nabokov's ever-changing world and the cultural effects generated by the intersection of the historical and geographical coordinates of his journey are connected with his interest in the multi-colored world of insects. Critics have deeply analyzed Nabokov's passion for lepidoptera, which he often hints at in *Speak, Memory*, and their connections with his fictional world. His interest in this world and the natural mysteries that it hides cannot be separated from his multicultural

---

[72] As regards Mademoiselle's caricature and her difficulties, it is interesting what Delage-Toriel (2017, 218–219) claims, "Is Nabokov's embodiment of Mademoiselle most moving when it is, paradoxically, the least incarnate? Let us rather say that Nabokov is probably most appealing when his most personal concerns coincide with her character, even when his self-protective strategy or reflex (most often in English) leads him to mitigate the inevitable poignancy of the situation with some form of distancing burlesque. This is the case each time the governess is compared to a bird. She is first referred to as a lone bird, whose leitmotif cry [...] is '*gdie*' ('where'), the single Russian word she has registered. [...] Mademoiselle's raucous cry signals a form of uprootedness that is not merely geographic, nor even cultural, but properly psychological. Even after she has returned to Switzerland, Mademoiselle continues to long for an imagined Eldorado, now turning Russia, [...] into a Paradise lost." Although Nabokov considers himself an American in an interview and claims "I am as American as April in Arizona," he adds "I owe too much to the Russian language and landscape to be emotionally involved in, say, American regional literature, or Indian dances, or pumpkin pie on a spiritual plane; but I do feel a suffusion of warm, lighthearted pride when I show my green USA passport at European frontiers" (Gold 2003, 200).

and plurilingual education (Boyd 2011, 73–105)[73]. Likewise, the metaphoric relationship between the changing aspects of insects and the ambiguous effects of plurilingualism is a *leitmotif* running through much of Brodsky's transnational poetry (Russo 2015, 82–94). Nabokov devotes a long section in the text to his memories of the insects that he found and examined in the Russian countryside during his childhood. In particular, he is charmed by the insects' fast process of transformation and camouflage, as the means they use to adapt to the changeable conditions of their environment. He emphasizes the "supernatural" effects of their mutable nature:

> Consider the imitation of oozing poison by bubblelike macules on a wing [...] or by glossy yellow knobs on a chrysalis [...]. Consider the tricks of an acrobatic caterpillar [...] which in infancy looks like bird's dung, but after molting develops scrabbly hymenopteroid appendages and baroque characteristics, allowing the extraordinary fellow to play two parts at once [...]. When a butterfly has to look like a leaf, not only are all the details of a leaf beautifully rendered but markings mimicking grub-bored holes are generously thrown in (124–125).

The magic of insects allows them to perform different parts in the theater of nature, and their natural skill in changing their features and colors seems to respond to their life as exiles, since they often have to adapt to the changes of the environment. Nabokov himself confirms that Darwin's theory of natural selection "[...] could not explain the miraculous coincidence of imitative aspect and imitative behaviour" (125). The inimitable imitative skill with which insects are endowed testifies to the presence in this world of things that man cannot explain. The lepidopteran *leitmotif* is thus used by Nabokov to demonstrate that, to quote Boyd (2011, 88), "[...] there is always more behind things – beyond our human sense of space and time, beyond the limits of personality and mortality." As to the foreign phrases and sentences in the text, the link between the physical features of insects, like the spots and colors that decorate the butterflies' wings, and the use of the different linguistic codes, mostly in the form of "fragments," is evident. The numerous foreignisms in the text raise new issues to disentangle; they express Nabokov's different moments of being and his new cultural and linguistic identities. The French and Russian words and expressions are associated with the writer's stages and "camouflage" his double or triple identity in the international context of Western Europe. The foreign phrases are the narrative reminders of a linguistic "multiverse" to question. The foreign words, which are often translated into the target language, blur the time borders and, at the same time, merge into the text. The author tries to join the linguistic geography of his past in his homeland and in Europe and does so by manipulating the

---

73 Nabokov declares in an interview that "[...] had there been no revolution in Russia, I would have devoted myself entirely to lepidopterology and never written any novels at all" (*Ivi*, 201).

time constraints. Nabokov confirms the "blurring" power of butterflies: "I confess I do not believe in time. [...] the highest enjoyment of timelessness [...] is when I stand among rare butterflies and their food plants" (139). The natural "devices" of butterflies, i.e. their colors, the spots on their wings, their metamorphosis and camouflage confuse the predators and are the metaphorical elements that, in Nabokov's writing, create the different linguistic "expressions" of his culturally variegated background.

The writer borrows from nature the tools with which he expresses the ambiguities generated by the rootless life of a wandering being, be it an insect or a man. The fading and changing effect of the natural devices modifies the Nabokovian geographies, represented, in turn, in the vast space of the author's personal memories. He recalls the different places of the Western world and of his homeland, which superimpose "[...] the temporal dimensions of the past, the present, and the future" (Lyaskovets 2014, 2). The space-time extension of the autobiography reproduces a "collection" of pictures from the past and blurs the time limits; as a result of the different stages of the composition of the text, the writer resorts to proleptic and analeptic devices, which convey a sense of eternity, in that they "postpone" the end of the autobiography (Scura 2008, 403). The space-time overlap "slows down" the progress of the narration. At the same time, the interdialogic relationship among languages poses different questions. The Bergsonian time extension leads to many linguistic comparisons (Lyaskovets 2014, 2)[74]; the author examines the semantic and expressive power of certain phrases and words by conjuring up the languages of his childhood. He looks for confirmation in the prismatic spaces of his plurilingual world, thus making his autobiography "[...] the meeting point of an impersonal art form and a very personal life" (Diment 2005, 178). Nabokov inscribes the account of his life within the borders of a surreal world, where space and time, namely the geographical and historical coordinates of his life, recreate a plurilingual narrative world by means of their intersection.

4. The migrant writer as "homo viator"

As seen, Nabokov was tutored by different Eastern European teachers. A Ukrainian tutor stayed at the Nabokovs in the winter of 1907–1908, then a Latvian arrived, soon followed by a Pole. Among the people that Nabokov quotes in

---

[74] Swan (2016, 22) compares Bergson's theory to human free will, as "Bergson believes that we have free will, and that the way we exercise it is through the internal qualitative experience of our own unique psychic states (duration-as-consciousness); moment of subjectivation. Duration is heterogeneous and qualitative, and if we are tuned into our internal sense of experience, then we can enact our free will."

Speak, Memory, Lensky is the Slavic tutor who, like Mademoiselle, deserves major attention. A protestant with Jewish origins (he succeeded the Pole), he was "versatile" (167), and Nabokov was surprised at "[...] how thoroughly he could explain anything related to our school studies" (167). He was a strict teacher and Nabokov quotes one of the most significant expressions that he uttered:

> Notwithstanding some of his oddities, he was really, a very pure, very decent human being, whose private principles were as strict as his grammar and whose bracing *diktantï* I recall with joy: *kolokololiteyshchiki perekolotili vïkarabkavshihsya vïhuholey*, 'the church-bell casters slaughtered the desmans that had scrambled out" (170).

Lenski's tongue twister is a focal point in the text from a linguistic perspective. On the "pretext" of describing Lenski and his strictness, Nabokov quotes a puzzling Russian phrase in his memories with his English translation. What is astonishing about the long phrase is the presence of alliteration, with the repetition of different sound effects, partially reproduced in the writer's English translation. Such foreign phrases, as seen, unexpectedly appear throughout the text, but the one that Lenski utters is characterized by its unpronounceable sounds. The length of the tongue twister responds to the narrative plan to expand the chronotopic space of the text and to emphasize, once again, the complex passage from the source language to the target language (Rothermel 2014, 134). The author's attempt to reproduce the sound effects in the target language shows that he does not mean to relinquish his source language[75]. Nabokov says that, some years later, he quoted in New York "[...] that tongue twister to a zoologist who had asked me if Russian was as difficult as commonly supposed" (170). Nabokov "transplants" his Russian background into the American context by means of his imaginary dislocations.

The writer goes back in time in chapter seven; this part of the text underscores how slow his progress to the USA is, since he returns once again to his homeland. Such slowness seems to extend the distance from the American horizons. This time, Nabokov does not illustrate an imaginary dislocation, but writes about a long journey, in the early years of the 20th century, with his family, from Saint Petersburg to Paris, by "The then great and glamorous Nord-Express" (141). The train becomes an emblematic means of transport and retraces Nabokov's thoughts and reflections. It extends his stay in Europe and conjures up his most intimate moments. The train is actually a narrative device, which is used to "postpone" the author's arrival in the USA; it is the image the narrator uses to create historical dislocations and recall different geographical places. Nabokov "delays" his journey to "fill in" the puzzle of his past with as many memories as

---

75 Wanner (2017, 82) claims that "The experience of loss associated with the impossibility of creating a perfect self-translation can serve as an emblem of Nabokov's own exilic condition."

he can. A symbolic object in this section is an old "valise" (143), a suitcase, which he carries with him during his journeys. Nabokov himself writes: "The fact that of our Russian heritage the hardiest survivor proved to be a traveling bag is both logical and emblematic" (143). Nabokov takes his suitcase with him wherever he goes. By interfering with time and extending it, to dwell on different past moments, the writer generates flashbacks. At the beginning of chapter eight, Nabokov "reintroduces" himself and his brother. At the beginning of the ninth chapter he outlines his autobiographical background and mentions his father's main events who, "Till the age of thirteen […] was educated at home by French and English governesses and by Russian and German tutors" (173). Since the use of the past simple makes the text realistic, Nabokov stresses the similarity between his father's background and his own. When he recalls his father, for example, he employs the third-person singular pronoun and points out the bond between "I" and "he." If the third-person singular pronoun lends itself to a higher degree of fictionalization, following the barthesian theoretical approach, Nabokov employs, in this case, such a pronoun to underscore the reality of his being and the influence it received from his father. By associating the third-person singular pronoun (which refers to his father) with his past and history, he highlights his family ties. At the same time, he gradually depicts an independent *ego*. The steady return to different space-time levels creates narrative "fragments" which make the writer, as Cesereanu (2006, 34) explains, "[…] untied from domestic spaces, from territories, freed from the geography of his homeland […], and actually feeling unchained from the entire geography of a sick Europe." Even before travelling to the USA, the writer loses his fixed abode in the European space and retraces his route as a *homo viator*, a man in transition throughout the complex history of his geographical puzzle. Nabokov's passage from one country to another in the old continent decomposes his self. By illustrating, in *Speak, Memory*, the relationship between text and context, Nabokov "collects" the different parts of his *ego* and paves the way for a process of cultural and linguistic readjustment, characterized by the ceaseless interaction between his Russian and European identities.

The geographical setting goes on changing and the narrative map of the text takes the reader to Berlin in the tenth chapter, where Nabokov spent some months at the end of 1910 with his tutor Lenski. In the German atmosphere, the writer is introduced to American culture, when he goes to the Wintergarten Theatre to see the American Gala Girls, whose dance stirs Nabokov's erotic associations with the New World and is a possible inspiration for *Lolita* (1955). The author's discussion with his father about this unusual experience "stages" an interesting plurilingual moment. When Nabokov's father tells his son about his sexual fantasies generated by the view of those dancers, he says: " 'That, my boy, is just another of nature's absurd combinations, like shame and blushes, or grief and red eyes.' *"Tolstoy vient de mourir,"* (207). His wife's comment on this statement is an attempt to "censure" it: "'*Da chto tï* [something like "good gracious]!' [...] '*Pora domoy* [Time to go home],'" (207-208). The woman's Russian phrases seem to "suppress" any dream of moving overseas and her suggestion that they should go home sounds like a nostalgic moment, a "warning" that their home is in Russia. The geographical dislocation continues and the author switches the setting to Vyra, in Russia, where his family estate was located. Nabokov dwells on the colors of the wonderful sunsets that he could admire in his childhood estate, where "A colossal shadow would begin to invade the fields, and the telegraph poles hummed in the stillness" (212). The memory of the Russian sunsets is a moment of inspiration that, starting from the geographical setting of the wide Russian countryside, provides the author with the creativity to write lines and test his plurilingual poetry writing. He often makes references to the places where he spends his childhood. It is during his summer stays in the countryside when he takes up, at fourteen, the difficult art of versification. As he remembers his first experiments with creating poetry, he writes: "My medium happened to be Russian, but could have been just as well Ukrainian, or Basic English, or Volapük. The kind of poem I produced in those days was hardly anything more than a sign I made of being alive" (217). Although the language used by the writer for his versification is Russian, he does not hide his difficulties. What is remarkable about his first attempts at versification is the fact that, "[...] the Russian elegy suffered from a bad case of verbal anemia" (219). Poetry writing turns out to be a linguistic experiment, which allows the writer to make his metalinguistic comments on the lexis of the languages he employs. Nabokov states that his mother tongue lacks suitable expressive means, but his inexperience seems to be the main reason for his difficulties in poetry writing:

> An innocent beginner, I fell into all the traps laid by the singing epithet. Not that I did not struggle. In fact, I was working at my elegy very hard, taking endless trouble over every line, choosing and rejecting, rolling the words on my tongue with the glazed-eyed solemnity of a tea-taster, and still it would come, that atrocious betrayal (220-221).

Nabokov the poet deals with the problems of composition and cannot go beyond the limits of the Russian literary tradition. In this regard, he quotes an example that is worth analyzing:

> The hackneyed order of words (short verb or pronoun – long adjective – short noun) engendered the hackneyed disorder of thought, and some such line as *poeta gorestnïe gryozï*, translatable and accented as 'the poet's melancholy daydreams,' led fatally to a rhyming line ending in *rozï* (roses) or *beryozï* (birches) or *grozï* (thunderstorms), so that certain emotions were connected with certain surroundings not by a free act of one's will but by the faded ribbon of tradition (221).

The art of versification becomes, by means of Nabokov's metalinguistic remarks, an act of translation, a "passage" from prose to poetry. The author dwells on his first approach to endolinguistic translation and, by carrying out his poetic experiments, tries to create a pluridiscursive narrative context, in order to "smooth," with the lexical interdialogism, the linguistic disharmonies generated by the interlingual translation of the numerous foreignisms (Jakobson 1959, 233). Nabokov's translation questions the devices of the Russian literary tradition, those "faded ribbons" that still make versification difficult. His effort consists in "cutting" the weakened ribbons of the past, in order to suggest new devices as a verse maker. To accomplish this innovative task, he seeks dialogue with the reality that he means to poeticize. As Bakhtin (1979, 139) states, the poetic word needs to devise the expressive means that best represent the object it intends to signify. Likewise, the writer tries to join the poetic word to the object that he means to associate with the lexical background of his poetry. Accordingly, he looks for a "dialogue" with the semiotic clues that refer to the object itself. In this attempt to change the poetic tradition, the poetic word, which, in the quoted passage is "gryozï," must necessarily rhyme with another word standing for nature. The poet cannot find another way to make it rhyme differently; however, the poet's dreams, the "gryozï," find a dialogic compromise with "rozï," "beryozï" and "grozï," in that his dreams are generated by the natural elements. Nabokov exemplifies a case, which required much perspicacity and ability to communicate with the lexis of different registers.

Nabokov points out the end of the century changes in versification and dwells on metre and on the composition of Russian poetry. His reflections allow him to examine the semantic value of certain Russian words, experiment with the phonic associations they evoke, and translate them into his target language by preserving their sound effects. Nabokov writes that "The rather monotonous designs into which early nineteenth-century Russian poets had twisted the pliant giant elegy resulted in certain words, or types of words [...] being coupled again and again, and this later lyricists could not shake off for a whole century" (220). In his "analysis" of Russian versification, he claims that "In an especially obsessive arrangement, peculiar to the iambic of four to six feet, a long, wriggly adjective would occupy the first four or five syllables of the last three feet of the line" (220). He explains this statement as follows:

> A good tetrametric example would be *ter-pi bes-chis-len-nï-e mu-ki* (en-dure in-cal-cu-la-ble tor-ments). The young Russian poet was liable to slide with fatal ease into this alluring abyss of syllables, for the illustration of which I have chosen *beschislennïe* only because it translates well; the real favorites were such typical elegiac components as *zadumchivïe* (pensive), *utrachennïe* (lost), *muchitel'nïe* (anguished), and so forth, all accented on the second syllable (220).

Nabokov translates the Russian syllables into English as well: "(*nï* in the Russian example, 'la' in the English one)" (220). Such experiments are examples of "linguistic alloys," namely combinations of different linguistic components, which develop the dialogue between two or more languages (Maklakova, Khovanskaya, Grigorieva 2017, 1264). The creation of the "linguistic alloy" in Nabokov's text "[...] is connected with the interest of the writer in the language as it is, be it his native or a foreign language. He is eager to experiment with new language expressive means" (*Ibid.*). The imaginary space of Nabokov's private history exerts its influence over the linguistic stratification of verse writing.

In the twelfth chapter of the autobiography Nabokov switches to a real historical setting, threatened by the winds of war of Lenin's Regime. It is one of the few sections in which the author outlines the historical background of his time and describes the first steps of his family's exile. These pages illustrate Nabokov's geographical itinerary, in contrast to the previous chapters, which dwell on the writer's metaphorical and imaginary route. Nabokov provides some historical references at the end of 1917, when "Lenin took over, [...] and a regime of bloodshed, concentration camps, and hostages entered upon its stupendous career" (241). The romantic tones of the imaginary history of the autobiography suddenly change and the account becomes more realistic and dramatic. Nabokov and his brother are sent to Crimea by their father and, once again, the journey by train becomes a moment of long expectations. This important historical moment illustrates the effects of Nabokov's first geographical dislocation before moving to Europe. When he is forced to move to Crimea, which "[...] seemed completely foreign" (244), Nabokov shows the first blunt "[...] pangs of exile" (244). The threats of the Russian Civil War stand out when Nabokov remembers the men who were shot by the Bolsheviks (the latter had come from Sebastopol with the purpose of killing their opponents in Crimea). As he mentions the fight between the Red Army and the White Army, the writer recalls his romantic past in his estate in Saint Petersburg and his love for Tamara. If the real dimension of history retraces the different steps of his itinerary, the idealised dimension of his past represents a pretext for analyzing the elements of his plurilingual world. When he quotes some lines written in one of Tamara's letters to him, he makes some contrastive comparisons:

> 'Why did we feel so cheerful when it rained?' she asked in one of her last letters, reverting as it were to the pure source of rhetorics. '*Bozhe moy*' (*mon Dieu* – rather than 'My God'), where has it gone, all that distant, bright, endearing (*Vsyo eto dalyokoe, svetloe, miloe* – in Russian no subject is needed here, since these are neuter adjectives that play the part of abstract nouns, on a bare stage, in a subdued light) (249).

Once again, Nabokov employs three languages in this passage to evoke his past. He switches from "*Bozhe moy*," his source language, to "My God," his target language, by means of the French "*mon Dieu*," which can be viewed as his language of transition. Nabokov's translation exercises in *Speak, Memory* reveal a process of foreignization. Translating the autobiography means "crossing" the linguistic borders of the geographical spaces along his route to the USA[76]. Foreignizing means explicating and illustrating how the writer's message is translated from the source language into the target language, through the "mediating" language, French, thus generating a sense of "estrangement" in the reader. Such a complex process of translation, which, as seen, unveils the estranging route of different linguistic spaces, involves "[…] reflexivity – that is, awareness of the text's condition as translation" (Kadiu 2019, 36–37). In addition, reflexivity "[…] is possible only if we make visible the act of translating itself, by showing the original text that is being translated" (Kadiu 2019, 36–37). By dwelling on the various linguistic "steps" of his translation, Nabokov involves the bilingual/plurilingual reader in his choices of translation. The work is not only a plurilingual account of the writer's life abroad, but is also the narrative "laboratory" that he creates to experiment with the translation of the different linguistic sounds from the source language into the target language. Nabokov centers on the hybrid dimension characterized by the dialogue among languages. According to Kadiu (2019, 38), "[…] the 'otherness' of the foreign text cannot be made visible without simultaneously releasing the violent act of erasure and substitution that the translating process operates." Nabokov's self-translation of the numerous foreign sentences in his autobiography unfolds the processes of "violation" and "annihilation" that the structures of the source language undergo. The elimination and the consequent substitution of the pre-existing structures turns out to be an attempt to "come to terms" with the target language.

The concept of reflexivity is helpful in this regard; Nabokov looks for an interlingual dialogue by means of two different aspects that pertain to reflexivity. Reflexivity can be hermeneutic or mechanical: hermeneutic reflexivity is "[…] the translator's subjective interpretation of the source text," whereas mechanical reflexivity is "[…] a thoughtless, automatic response to a stimulus" (Kadiu 2019, 10). In his search for a dialogue with the languages he uses, Nabokov, as a writer and translator, applies both hermeneutic reflexivity and mechanical reflexivity, although he adapts mechanical reflexivity to his own linguistic needs and decreases its "mechanical" aspect. In his analysis of Russian and English metre, he, as seen, often tries to find the most suitable translation of the single syllables and words. The steady interaction among the single units of the source language and of the target language allows him to create the target text and compose and recompose the linguistic puzzle of versification. From this perspective, Nabokov

---

76 As regards the concept of the passage through borders and frontiers, see also Hamrit 2019, 277–280.

establishes a subjective relationship with the target language, in that he "discusses" the meanings with it, he "dialogues" with the target language and often translates the linguistic units through the lenses of his personal and cultural sphere. At the same time, he analyzes the semantic aspects of the words he translates. Nabokov turns to mechanical reflexivity when he translates verses and syllables, since he examines the "technical" characteristics of poetry and metre. However, he avoids, at the same time, a mechanical and depersonalized translation, by adapting the "fragments" of the source language to the background of the target text and translating them into English. He involves the reader in the process of translation and "accompanies" him or her through the stages of translation[77].

In this analysis of Nabokov's autobiography, I have taken for granted, as critics have always claimed, that Russian and English in *Speak, Memory* are, respectively, the source and the target languages. However, Nabokov's mastery of his ever-claimed target language, English, reverses the roles of the two languages. The constant self-translation of Russian phrases into English and vice versa, blurs the identity of both source and target languages, by "transferring" the sense of foreignness from one language to another. On the one hand, Nabokov employs Russian in-between the English lines; Russian underlies the whole text, which is conceived in Nabokov's source language and is written in his target language. Therefore, Russian often emerges in the text in order to recall the past and "slow down" the storyline. Having the purpose of reminding the reader of the author's origins, Russian is used with the adopted language[78]. Nabokov "places" the two languages between two mirrors and makes a playful use of them, thus turning the source language into the target language and vice versa. Nabokov self-translates some phrases into Russian in the English macrotext, as if he were trying to improve the use of the two languages by repeating the experiments of self-translation. So, what is English to Nabokov? A target language, a translingual code of communication or a source language? English has all three "identities:" it

---

77 As Wilson (2009, 194) writes, "The self-translator constructs a new reality by deconstructing both source and target language. The losses and gains in the passage between the source and the target language and the ensuing lack of precision take the writer into the realm of the inexpressible, the space where new expressions are generated in pursuit of the inner voice." In an old article, Steiner (1970, 126) points out "[…] the polysemic nature of Nabokov's uses of language[s]. […] the possible existence of a private mixed idiom 'beneath,' 'coming before' the localization of different languages in the articulate brain." Moreover, he states that "Nabokov is a writer who seems to me to work very near the intricate threshold of syntax; he experiences linguistic forms in a state of manifold potentiality and, moving across vernaculars, is able to keep words and phrases in a charged, unstable mode of vitality."

78 Voronina (2017, 45) claims that "Nabokov's 'metamorphosis' into an American writer might be 'atrocious,' but it was obviously not undergone at the expense of the reader. The author's pain, in this work as well as in many others, is our gain – a beautiful illusion of perfection that we long to believe in."

is the target language at the beginning of the writer's emigration, it is the writer's translingual means of communication, as a lingua franca he uses in a foreign context, and becomes the source language when the writer settles in the USA. Nabokov's autobiography has a didactic purpose as well[79]. He often uses a cryptic language and mainly addresses readers with an intimate knowledge of English and Russian, by involving them in the complex task of sharing the exercises of self-translation. To a monolingual reader, the text is but an account of the author's past.

Speak, Memory illustrates the writer's self both as the subject and the object of the text. As the subject, Nabokov's self is the "creator" of the work, the protagonist that tells about his past. As the object, Nabokov's self represents the writer's unconscious identity that is translated into different linguistic codes by the cultural contexts it goes through[80]. From a semiotic angle, following Lotman's theory (1985, 64), Nabokov's childhood and, therefore, the history of his self, lie in the central part of his semiospheric structure which preserves the foreign words and expressions of the past, whereas the linguistic systems of the second stage of his route are "located" along the edge of the semiospheric structure. The central area is more static, in that it has been rooted in the semiospheric structure since the writer's birth; the edge is more "dynamic" and interacts both with the outer world and with the center of the writer's semiosphere, thus generating continuous linguistic comparisons and examples of cultural and linguistic hybridism. Likewise, the author mirrors this process in *Speak, Memory:* Russian is located at the center of the writer's semiosphere and some words and phrases of the source language are introduced into the English macrotext, which lies along the edge of Nabokov's semiospheric structure. Such words and phrases establish relationships of intersemiotic exchanges with the target language. The "osmotic" process, generated by the dialogue among different places, moulds the writer's plurilingual literary world. The relentless introduction of the foreign elements into the writer's linguistic system creates a space of attrition (Schmid and Köpke 2017, 637–667), where the elements of the mother tongue clash with the ones of other languages and form explosive moments of new linguistic and cultural meanings.

---

79 As regards educational and didactic autobiographies, see Kuek, Ling 2017, 284. See also the comparisons between English and Russian in Nabokov's essay "On Learning Russian" (Boyd and Tolstoy 2019, 220–223).

80 As regards self-translation, Wanner (2018, 122) claims that "The term 'self-translation' is in itself ambiguous, depending on whether we see the 'self' as the subject or the object of the translational process. If seen as the subject, the self is the agent of textual production. If the self is perceived as the object, however, self-translation literally involves a 'translation of the self.'"

5. *Look at the Harlequins!* A sequel to *Speak, Memory*

In this study of four Russian-American "fugitive" writers, Nabokov deserves more space and major attention, as his autobiography continues in *Look at the Harlequins!*, published three years before his death. It is known, among Nabokov's scholars, that most of his novels and stories (not to say all of them) can be read from an autobiographical perspective through their protagonists, the latter being Nabokov's *alter egos*. Unlike other novels written during his American years, *Look at the Harlequins!* has been regarded as a minor work by critics (Springer 2002, 360)[81]. In it, Nabokov illustrates and re-maps his life by "employing" the protagonist Vadim Vadimovich N. (VV) to split his *persona*, look at himself from another angle and portray his life through the voice of a fictional character. As Springer claims (*Ibid.*), "Practically all the details of the novel's settings and plot, the life and characteristics of the narrator and the numerous other characters in the book are modelled on Nabokov's writings and life[82]." While *Speak, Memory* is Nabokov's real autobiography, narrated in the first-person singular pronoun, *Look at the Harlequins!* is his fictional autobiography, since it maps out his route from Russia to the USA through Western Europe, by means of his *Doppelgänger* VV. The work has been given little consideration from a diegetic and a linguistic point of view. As to the themes of the work, some critics, like Nafisi (2019, 55), have recently pointed out that the book is "[…] the mock memoir of a Russian émigré writer, Vadim Vadimovich. […] Vadim Vadimovich recounts the story of his life […], and there's no evident trace of the narrator's creator. But […], we find more of Nabokov's presence in *Look at the Harlequins!* than in any other of his novels." Nabokov hides his identity behind his bizarre protagonist; he shares with him a similar name, the year of birth, the emigration to Western Europe after the Russian Revolution, the Cambridge years from 1919 to 1922, the long stay in Western Europe in the émigré circles and the emigration to America. *Look at the Harlequins!* reads like the sequel to *Speak, Memory*, as it "reconsiders" the writer's route and even extends it overseas and back to Russia. It is Nabokov's fictitious story, based on his imaginary memoirs in the country of emigration and in the motherland[83]. The author imagines, in this work, his life in America and his return to his motherland.

---

[81] As Boyd (1991, 655) writes, "While many thought *Ada*'s exuberance revealed a failure of both moral insight and artistic control, *Transparent Things* disconcerted by its uncompromising sparseness, and *Look at the Harlequins!* by its apparent narcissism."

[82] According to Boyd (1990, 253), "[…] the narrator and central character of *Look at the Harlequins!*, is a Russo-American novelist whose name, career, and oeuvre plainly parallel those of his maker."

[83] In this regard, Nabokov shows some contradictions: on the one hand, he has his protagonist go back to Russia and, therefore, conveys his nostalgia for his country; on the other hand,

Speak, Memory and *Look at the Harlequins!* have a similar diegetic organization, in which the French and Russian substrates are often revealed in the English macrotext. I will not focus on the plot, which, however, deserves only few lines to realize that Nabokov sets the story in a plurilingual context. After moving to Western Europe from Saint Petersburg, VV marries Iris, whom he met in France. Iris is killed by a suitor and VV marries Annette, his secretary, with whom he has a daughter, Bel. When Annette divorces from VV, Bel chooses to live with her mother. However, Annette dies (she drowns) and Bel goes to live with VV. The latter marries Louise, but Bel takes a dislike for her father's new wife and goes to Russia with an American left-winged man. VV leaves for Russia to vainly look for his daughter. In the end, he marries a young woman, Bel's former classmate, who is never given a name, and is both his real love and the reader. VV addresses her as "You." Nabokov has his *alter ego* deal with the problems of translation. The foreign expressions are not translated literally, but the protagonist makes frequent metatextual comments in his translation. One of the first comparative passages of the text is a poem that VV wrote for his beloved Iris. The protagonist translates the poem into English for his lover by commenting on his translation. As regards the title, "Vlyublyonnost'," the narrator says that it "[...] puts in a golden nutshell what English needs three words to express" (Nabokov 2017, 21)[84] since its English translation is *"being in love"* (Nabokov 2012, 39)[85]. In this case, Nabokov highlights that, compared with English, the structures of the Russian language are more concise. The whole poem reads as follows:

My zabyváem chto vlyublyónnost'
Ne prósto povorót litsá,
A pod kupávami bezdónnost',
Nochnáya pánika plovtsá.

Pokúda snítsya, snís', vlyublyónnost',
No probuzhdéniem ne múch',
I lúchshe nedogovoryónnost'
Chem éta shchél' i étot lúch.

Nabokov states in *Strong Opinions* (1990, 9) that he would have never returned to Russia: "*Would you ever go back to Russia?* I will never go back, for the simple reason that all the Russia I need is always with me: literature, language, and my own Russian childhood. I will never return. I will never surrender. [...] In America I'm happier than in any other country. It is in America that I found my best readers, minds that are closest to mine. I feel intellectually at home in America. It is a second home in the true sense of the word."

84 All subsequent quotations from *Look at the Harlequins!* will refer to this edition; page numbers are given parenthetically in the text.

85 The English translation of the title of VV's poem is not quoted in Nabokov's text, but is provided in the Italian translation of the novel (see bibliography).

Napomináyu chto vlyublyónnost'
Ne yáv', chto métiny ne té,
Chto mózhet-byt' potustorónnost'
Priotvorílas' v temnoté (21).

When Iris asks VV to translate the poem into English, he explains his translation to her:

> It goes like this. We forget – or rather tend to forget – that being in love (*vlyublyonnost'*) does not depend on the facial angle of the loved one, but is a bottomless spot under the nenuphars, *a swimmer's panic in the night* (here the iambic tetrameter happens to be rendered – last line of the first stanza, *nochnáya pánika plovtsá*). Next stanza: While the dreaming is good – in the sense of "while the going is good" – do keep appearing to us in our dreams, *vlyublyonnost'*, but do not torment us by waking us up or telling too much: reticence is better than that chink and that moonbeam. Now comes the last stanza of this philosophical love poem (22).

Once again, as occurs in *Speak, Memory*, VV, alias Nabokov, shows the complex structures of metatranslation, since he is willing to disclose every step of his choices of translation, especially when he writes verse. When he explains his translation to Iris, VV apologizes to her for not having been able to create the iambic tetrameter in the last line of the first stanza of the source text. In my discussion of the self-translation of the Russian and French words in *Speak, Memory*, I claimed that Nabokov complies with the principle of the hermeneutic reflexivity. Likewise, the author adopts the same approach in his sequel, "dialogues" with the source texts of the passages that he translates in the story and renders the phonic and syntactic features of the target language. The writer's comments in his translation of the poem aim to provide Iris and, therefore, the reader, with some clues about the different stanzas that he translates. Such comments express the writer's effort to communicate with his addressee, who is, in this case, Iris. He means to draw her attention and to involve her and the reader in his process of translation. Before translating the third stanza, VV claims that the poem is a "Philosophical love poem" (22), and goes on with his translation: "*Napomináyu*, I remind you, that *vlyublyonnost'* is not wide-awake reality, that the markings are not the same (a moon-striped ceiling, *polosatyy ot luny potolok*, is, for instance, not the same kind of reality as a ceiling by day), and that, maybe, the hereafter stands slightly ajar in the dark" (22). In the translation of the third stanza, VV is even more exhaustive and gives more explanations to account for his choices of translation. In his "commented" translation of the second stanza, VV seems to look back for inspiration to the Shakespearean *motif* of sleep and its illusive powers to soothe man's evils. In the last stanza, in particular, the writer-translator's "presence" is more evident, in that he translates the single words of the poem and paraphrases the lines explaining the meaning of the title, "*Vlyu-*

blyonnost'." It epitomizes human conscience as well as other aspects of reality. VV, in fact, includes, in his paraphrastic translation, a metaphor, which is used to point out the different aspects and meanings that any object, like a ceiling, assumes in the morning and at night. Although Nabokov recognizes, in the foreword to the English translation of *Eugene Onegin* (1975, viii), the effectiveness of literal translation only, he employs the paraphrastic approach, as well, to boost the interdialogism between English and Russian[86]. Nabokov uses a paraphrastic translation in this poem, since he is not (from the perspective of the novel) the "real" translator, but renders the source text through the protagonist's voice. Nabokov's translation is somehow "mediated" and "interpreted" by VV; it needs, therefore, further explanations, explications, to make the reader familiar with the messages and the metaphors of the source text.

6. Linguistic plays in the paraphrastic mosaic

Look at the Harlequins! is not only structured by comparing the lexical aspect of the languages that the author uses, but is also based on certain "linguistic challenges" among the characters. In *Speak, Memory*, Nabokov's employment of the two (and sometimes three) languages is characterized by the author's constant presence in the text, in order to explicate, mostly using a literal approach, the foreign "fragments" and units that appear in the plurilingual conversations among the characters. In *Look at the Harlequins!*, Nabokov, instead, frequently adopts a paraphrastic translation, since he avoids translating some situational conversations among the characters and "reports" their dialogues in the target language. When he tells of a dinner that VV is having in Paris with his wife Iris and his brother-in-law, Ivor, he dwells on a short plurilingual dialogue. The author does not translate such a dialogue, but explains it in the target language. Before going to the dinner, VV goes to a store to buy some olives, and runs into a certain Lieutenant Starov. The narrator explains the short conversation between them as follows: " 'Pleasant meeting!' he went on in his curious English (not parading it as might have seemed but using it by unconscious association). [...] I bought my olives, replying the while, in Russian, that, yes, my wife and I were dining out" (55). And when VV, his wife and Ivor take a taxi to go to the restaurant, Ivor says to VV: " 'Good to see you, old boy,' he said to me, with a distinct American intonation (which I shyly imitated at dinner until he growled: 'Very funny')" (55). The protagonist does not quote the words actually used by

---

[86] In this regard, Shvabrin (2019, 338) writes that "The determined literalist continued to engage in the paraphrastic translation of poetry into poetry at the same time as he argued against the advisability, indeed legitimacy, of such an approach."

the protagonists, but "sums up" what they say and employs the target language to provide the reader with some paralinguistic information, i. e. the accent and the intonation used by the speakers. VV uses a discursive, argumentative approach to translation in these dialogues, in that he does not analyze the words that he translates, but resorts to English to depict the paralinguistic aspects of the conversations.

Nabokov's biographical elements come to light in the narrator's educational route. VV reads English and Russian books and shares with the author the same plurilingual background. His itinerary from Russia to America is similar to Nabokov's, as explained, and constitutes his linguistic evolution from Russian to English. VV spent in Cambridge the same years as Nabokov did, from 1919 to 1922, and claims that "[…] my domestic language was English, while the body of my own Russian works started to grow" (104). Cambridge is the first English-speaking city along VV's route. It is the context where he expresses his comments on his linguistic passage, thus unfolding the author's doubts about his knowledge of the target language. After moving to Paris, he is aware of his linguistic in-betweenness:

> […] the question confronting me in Paris, in the late Thirties, was precisely could I fight off the formula and rip up the ready-made, and switch from my glorious self-developed Russian, not to the dead leaden English of the high seas with dummies in sailor suits, but an English I alone would be responsible for, in all its new ripples and changing light? (104).

VV intends to learn an English of his own, a "personalized" form of English, rejecting, at the same time, the English that every emigrant learns. He does not mean to learn English as a lingua franca, "contaminated" by the emigrants' accents and cultural influences; he means to be proficient in English and become a translingual writer. His linguistic doubts stand out during his crossing to America: "I wish to dwell mercilessly on a situation that was bad enough before I left Europe but almost killed me during the crossing" (104). The sea is a space in-between two continents and languages, it is a thought-provoking natural element and flattens the passengers' cultural differences. During his voyage, the emigrant reflects on his mother tongue and his adopted language. In this regard, VV says:

> Russian and English had existed for years in my mind as two worlds detached from one another. (It is only today that some interspatial contact has been established: 'A knowledge of Russian, […], will help you to relish much of the wordplay in the most English of the author's English novels; consider for instance this: 'The champ and the chimp came all the way from Omsk to Neochomsk.' What a delightful link between a real round place and 'ni-o-chyom,' the About-Nothing land of modern philosophic linguistics!') I was acutely aware of the syntactic gulf separating their sentence structures (104).

The transoceanic crossing "connects" the narrator's source and target languages, which he had always seen as two separated and different entities. The "interspatial contact" is generated by the passage and by the emigrating experience that he shares with the other passengers on board the ship. As a consequence of this interlingual communication, VV realizes that a connection between his mother tongue and English is necessary. Russian turns out to be essential to be able to understand and master the target language, although the protagonist recognizes the remarkable difference between the two languages[87]. The connection between English and Russian leads to a contrastive comparison between their stylistic and syntactic features:

> I feared (unreasonably, as was to transpire eventually) that my allegiance to Russian grammar might interfere with an apostatical courtship. Take tenses: how different their elaborate and strict minuet in English from the free and fluid interplay between the present and the past in their Russian counterpart (which Ian Bunyan has so amusingly compared in last Sunday's MYT to 'a dance of the veil performed by a plump graceful lady in a circle of cheering drunks'). The fantastic number of natural-looking nouns that the British and Americans apply in lovely technical senses to very specific objects also distressed me (104).

In his comparison between the two languages, English mirrors its speakers' "strictness" as opposed to the stylistic characteristics of Russian, which lends itself, according to VV, to alliterative sounds and puns and is, therefore, the language of art. The "strictness" that marks English stands out in the use of particular nouns that refer to specific objects and situations, and whose translation into other languages is not always possible. Nabokov often resorts to the epistolary means to convey his difficulty in learning the target language. When Iris asks VV to read a letter she means to include in the story she is writing, he is impressed by her skill in imitating the mistakes that a Russian speaker would make when writing in English. The author of the letter is, in the story, a Frenchman, Jules, who writes love letters to the English Diana Vane, since he mistakes her for his former lover. According to Iris's narrative plan, this letter had to be written by Jules in a foreigner's English. Here is an excerpt from the letter:

> [...] I love you more than life – more than two lives, your and my, together taken. Are you not ill? Or maybe you have found another? Another lover, yes? [...] My supplication is modest and just. Give only one more interview to me! One interview! I am prepared to

---

[87] The dialogue between Nabokov's source and target languages is important to "survive" the consequences of emigration. As Nafisi (2019, 47–48) writes, "Nabokov lost his mother tongue and his fatherland. Yet he never succumbed to the role of victim, even while suffering the void of exile. He was unwilling to surrender himself to the coercion of exile. And on a deeper level, neither would he yield to the coercion of fatalism of time [...]." It is interesting to notice that Nafisi uses the word "fatherland," which stresses the "masculine" identity of Nabokov's native country.

meet with you it does not matter where – on the street, in some café, in the Forest of Boulogne – but I must see you, must speak with you and open to you many mysteries before I will die. Oh, this is no threat! I swear that if our interview will lead to a positive result, if, otherwise speaking, you will permit me to hope, only to hope, then, oh then, I will consent to wait a little. But you must reply to me without retardment, my cruel, stupid, adored little girl!

Your Jules (52)

The letter is the means that Nabokov uses to examine the most common mistakes that could be made in the translation from Russian into English. The epistolary style, as a "parallel" narrative dimension, is the narrative "counterpart" that allows him to express his linguistic doubts. It is the author's stream of consciousness, which overtly declares his linguistic problems. In addition, the letter is part of the hypotext, a hidden narrative space where the author is free to write about his difficulties with English, even though, bearing in mind that *Look at the Harlequins!* was written few years before Nabokov's death, he must have been proficient in English when the work was published. Nabokov relies on the device of the *myse en abyme*, the text within the text, to disclose his thoughts that still worry him, from a linguistic point of view, after living abroad for entire decades. By "digging" into the structure of the English macrotext, the author shows his concern with the doubts generated by the process of translation.

Nabokov "makes use" of VV to formulate contrastive comments on the two languages and expresses his thoughts about his condition as an exile. As is known, Nabokov never returned to Russia and, as a result, he could not write, unlike other émigrés who visited Russia, about the changes which took place in his motherland after being away for years. Many emigrant writers who returned to Russia, such as Cournos and Shteyngart, were "dismayed" by the "reversed" culture shock, owing to the backwardness of Russian life, as opposed to the wealthier conditions that they found in the English-speaking countries. However, in *Look at the Harlequins!*, Nabokov relies on VV's observations, since the author has him go back to Russia and, through his character's eyes, tries to imagine what Russia could be like after more than fifty years. Like Cournos and, as we will see, Shteyngart, VV is ironical about the description of the "newly-discovered" Russia. Nabokov has his character fly back to Leningrad and, when he returns to his city, he underlines the gloomy atmosphere and the backwardness, which the writer was probably acquainted with, as a consequence of the accounts of other Russian émigrés. VV observes:

[...] I had never seen my native city in June or July. Its aspect, therefore, evoked no thrill of recognition; it was an unfamiliar, if not utterly foreign, town, still lingering in some other era: an undefinable era, not exactly remote, but certainly the invention of body deodorants. [...] I was to remain only a couple of days in Leningrad and had not the time to get used to those infinitely sad emanations. [...] To be quite honest, only the dogs, the pigeons, the horses, and the very old, very meek cloakroom attendants seemed familiar to me" (178–179).

Nabokov imagines being back in Russia and seeing, through the protagonist of his novel, Leningrad's unrecognisable urbanscape. VV points out that the city has not progressed and that it has taken him back in time, not in a distant time, though. VV's return to Russia has the purpose of letting the writer figure out what it could be like to be back in his motherland as an exile after such a long time. The context of Leningrad oozes with the effects of the Regime and recalls Shteyngart's description of his return to Russia in *Little Failure*. In *Speak, Memory*, the author offers a rural portrait of his motherland, as he remembers his childhood years in his summer estate and, as regards the urban context, he gives a more "romantic" depiction, pervaded by the pale colors of the snow and the majesty of the city's buildings. The description that Nabokov gives or, better, imagines, of his city when he wrote *Look at the Harlequins!* in the 70s, is "updated" with the changes brought about by the advent of the Regime. Its effects are not only visible in the poverty that the writer sees when he imagines his return to Russia, but also in the control that the Regime imposes on people, especially in those areas that are more subject to foreign spies. When VV returns to Leningrad and describes his stay at the Astoria Hotel, he is shocked by the conditions of the hotel: "[…] a hideous pile built around World War One, I think. […]. The Iron Curtain is really a lampshade: its variety here was gemmed with glass incrustations in a puzzle of petals" (177). The writer's description of the hotel highlights the lack of modernization and the whole setting is dominated by the Soviet Regime: "The heavily bugged (I had been taught by Gay Gayley a way of finding that out in one gleeful twinkle) and therefore sheepish-looking room *'de luxe,'* […], did have a private bath as stipulated, but it took me some time to cope with a convulsive torrent of clay-colored water" (177). The presence of the bugs and the expression "The Iron Curtain" emphasize the author's awareness that the division between the East and the West is more than ever marked. Nabokov tests his knowledge of Russian and dwells, at the same time, on people's weird behaviour. In particular, when the *liftyorsha*, the elevator operator, addresses an old colleague of hers, she says: " '*Ya tebe eto popomnyu, sterva!* (I'll get even with you, dirty bitch)' […]" (177). When the elevator operator cannons into VV, she shouts at him: " '*Shtoy-ty suyoshsya pod nogi?* (Why do you get underfoot?)' she cried in the same insolent tone of voice […]" (178). Nabokov tests his source language in its original and natural context; he intends to make sure that his Russian still "works," that he can still use his source language both in the "unnatural" contexts of the English-speaking countries and in Russia. He tests his command of the two languages by translating into English the phrases that he quotes in Russian.

By having VV go to America, then to Russia and back to America, Nabokov dreams of visiting his country, as some émigrés did. This fictionalized autobiography thus illustrates the writer's transatlantic crossings and re-crossings that are not described in his original autobiography. He even imagines acting as a spy, when, while returning to the USA from Russia, he says to a passenger that he could not visit Leningrad's wonders because " 'I happen to be ,' [...] 'a triple agent and you know how it is' [...]" (182). The return to Russia is used by Nabokov to give a portrait of what life was like in his motherland in the years of the Cold War. The displacement in his native country, experienced through the protagonist of the story, is the consequence of a "metempsychotic" process, which takes him back to Russia. Nabokov describes his imaginary experience as a spy by means of his plurilingual dialogues with some compatriots during his journey from Russia to America, in particular with the poet Oleg Orlov. When the latter says to him: " *'Ekh*, Vadim Vadimovich *dorogoy* (dear), aren't you ashamed of deceiving our great warm-hearted country, our benevolent, credulous government, our overworked Intourist staff, in this nasty infantile manner! A Russian writer! Snooping! Incognito! [...]' " (184), VV replies to the poet's provocation with vehemence:

> 'What do you want, *merzavetz* (you scoundrel)?' [...] Nothing, nothing. Except to ruffle (*potormoshit'*) your conscience. Two courses presented themselves. We had to choose. [...]. Either to welcome you *po amerikanski* (the American way) with reporters, interviews, photographers, girls, garlands, [...]; or else to ignore you – and that's what we did. By the way: forged passports may be fun in detective stories, but our people are just not interested in passports. Aren't you sorry now? (184).

Nabokov imagines being considered a betrayer for having left his country. Therefore, he does not have his compatriots welcome VV on his return to Russia, where he is even accused of faking his documents. Oleg's bilingual dialogue goes on and French expressions are introduced too:

> *'Et ce n'est pas tout!'* he went on. 'Instead of writing for us, your compatriots, you, a Russian writer of genius, betray them by concocting, for your paymasters, *this* [...], this obscene novelette about little Lola or Lotte, whom some Austrian Jew or reformed pederast rapes after murdering her mother – no, excuse me – *marrying* mama first before murdering her – we like to legalize everything in the West, don't we, Vadim Vadimovich?' (185).

The author "trespasses" the borders of self-criticism and discusses his masterpiece *Lolita*. According to the passenger, who stands for the Russian institutions, the novel deals with scandalous issues and VV, *alias* Nabokov, "sells out" to the West, in order to make money. By having the passenger talk like this, Nabokov questions, towards the end of his career, his knowledge of the languages he speaks, as well as the morality of the topics he has chosen for his stories and novels. Oleg's accusations continue and VV reacts with anger:

> '*Vraiment?* And maybe you visited Leningrad merely to chat with a lady in pink under the lilacs? Because, you know, you and your friends are phenomenally naïve. The reason Mister [...] Vetrov was permitted to leave a certain labor camp in Vadim – odd coincidence – so he might fetch his wife, is that he has been cured now of his mystical mania – cured by such nutcrackers, such shrinkers as are absolutely unknown in the philosophy of your Western *sharlatany*. Oh yes, precious (*dragotsennyy*) Vadim Vadimovich -' (185).

The passenger clearly rejects the values of Western culture, now embodied by Nabokov, and even regards the Western scholars as charlatans. By involving the two characters in the conversation, Nabokov compares two different worlds and uses a straightforward language to describe the Western world, seen from the Eastern European perspective. If we take into account Todorov's (2014, 225) theories again about the relationships among cultures, the two characters' dialogue embodies the climax of the story, as it clearly contrasts two cultures from a praxeological perspective. As a consequence of their argument, they try to ignore each other, but such cultural disagreement leads to a brawl, as VV punches Oleg. The latter's answer still shows his courage and pride: " '*Nu, dali v mordu. Nu, tak chtozh?*' he muttered (Well, you've given me one in the mug. Well, what does it matter?). [...] '*Nu, dali,*' he repeated and presently wandered away" (185). The Russian expressions reveal Oleg's allegiance to his world, but Nabokov still translates them, showing that he does not mean to forget his mother tongue.

I have previously discussed that writing plays an important role in the author's linguistic education, and that his translations, stories and novels were tough, but useful exercises to improve his command of Russian, English and, partly, French. As *Look at the Harlequins!* "sums up" Nabokov's writing features, such as plurilingual dialogues and descriptions, puns, the *Doppelgänger*, "confused" identities and biographical elements, he includes in this story numerous metanarrative references to the imaginary works that VV wrote. Such works are the linguistic sources that fostered the fictional writer's plurilingual education. The linguistic labyrinth that the real author creates in this (and other) novels is emphasized by the symbolic use of mirrors, as heterotopic spaces which reflect another side of the protagonist's life, namely his identity in another imaginary dimension. The mirrors are also the images of the protagonist's cultural background, that is, his past. VV remembers a day when he looked at himself in the mirror, and "[...] saw the whole vista of my Russian books" (193). The books that VV sees are actually the writer's imaginary books, the books he would have liked to write, or parodic copies of his real books[88]. After claiming that *See under Real* is his first English novel, whose title partly recalls Nabokov's first novel in English, *The Real Life of Sebastian Knight*, he sees his Russian works through the "magic" mirror: "[...] *Tamara*, my first novel (1925) [...]. A grandmaster betrayed in *Pawn Takes Queen*. *Plenilune*, a moonburst of verse. *Camera Lucida*, the spy's mocking eye among the meek blind. The *Red Top Hat* of decapitation in a country of total injustice. And my best in the series: young poet writes prose on a *Dare*" (193). The protagonist then says that his Russian books "[...] had been gradually translated into English either by myself or under my direction, with my revisions" (194), and is proud to list some of his English books: "My English originals, headed by the fierce *See under Real* (1940), led through the changing light of *Esmeralda and Her Parandrus*, to the fun of *Dr. Olga Repnin* and the dream of *A Kingdom by the Sea*. There was also the collection of short stories *Exile from Mayda*, a distant island; and *Ardis*, [...]" (194)[89]. Like his author, VV deems his English writings to be qualitatively inferior to the Russian works, owing to his difficult passage from Russian to English.

I have more than once stated that *Look at the Harlequins!* is the sequel to *Speak, Memory* for various reasons. However, an important difference lies in the narrator's attitude to writing; Nabokov writes his "first" autobiography in the first-person singular pronoun and proves to be reliable, as he looks at the world from his own perspective. Although he might "contaminate" reality by introducing some personal views into the text, he gives an objective description of the facts, whereas, in *Look at the Harkequins!*, Nabokov entrusts VV with the task of relating the events. Accordingly, the reliability of the information may decrease, since it is presented through the perspective of another narrator. The latter, in fact, turns out, at the end of the book, to suffer from a not specified form of madness, and confesses he has suffered from mental disorders since his childhood. He gives unclear information about his conditions and the reader realizes that the whole story might not be entirely true. In the final part of the book, Vadim lingers on his problems and, being unable to move, finds himself stuck within the borders of space and time. The narrator's unreliability emerges

---

88 As Springer (2002, 367) claims, "A major theme of *Look at the Harlequins!*, [...], is that of writing. It accounts for the most brilliant and entertaining passages of the book, and it is here that Nabokov is at his most overtly self-parodic. Vadim's fictional novels are the main strategy used in *Look at the Harlequins!* to present the protagonist's status as an inferior copy of his author."

89 VV's works draw inspiration from Nabokov's novels and stories. Actually, "[...] Vadim struggles in vain for the ascendancy of being able to call himself its author: in the end, it is Nabokov's name that is written on the cover" (*Ivi*, 370). As regards the similar titles that VV's and Nabokov's books share, Nafisi (2019, 58) claims that "Each false rendition of a real title is nuanced and carries a coded message: Nabokov's *The Gift* becomes Vadim's *The Dare*, playing on the Russian word *dar*, meaning 'gift.' "

when, during his comatose state, he tries to recall his surname, which sounds like Nabokov. As often occurs in his previous novels, the real author gradually enters the text and unfolds his identity. Following Bakhtin's interpretation, Nabokov establishes an "ideological" relationship with his character, providing the reader with clues and sounds that lead to his name and surname; the author actually hides behind the protagonist (Bakhtin 1979, 142–143)[90]:

> […] I definitely felt my family name began with an *N* and bore an odious resemblance to the surname or pseudonym of a presumably notorious (Notorov? No) Bulgarian, or Babylonian, or, maybe, Betelgeusian writer with whom scatterbrained *émigrés* from some other galaxy constantly confused me; but whether it was something on the lines of Nebesnyy or Nabedrin or Nablidze (Nablidze? Funny) I simply could not tell. I preferred not to overtax my will power (go away, Naborcroft) and so gave up trying – or perhaps it began with a *B* and the *n* just clung to it like some desperate parasite? (210).

In his imaginary discourses with his unnamed lover, he draws his conclusions about time. The final part of his fictional autobiography looks into the nature of time and its irreversibility. The two autobiographies evoke the past and show the writer's effort to come to terms with it. Nabokov and VV try to interact with their past and cherish the illusion that it is retrievable and can still be part of the present. When VV thinks he has recovered from his mental disorders, he claims: "*Tak, vdol' naklónnogo luchá / Ya výshel iz paralichá. Along a slanting ray, like this / I slipped out of paralysis*" (211). However, his recovery is only illusory and so is his conviction that time can be reversed, as he says to his lover that "Time is not reversible. […] the notion of trying to twirl time is a *trouvaille*" (214).

Look at the Harlequins! is a mosaic of languages and cultures; it is a "Harlequin" that, once again, makes different people and places come together. The whole story originates from the well-known sentence that Nabokov's aunt once uttered: " 'Look at the harlequins!' […] All around you. Trees are harlequins, words are harlequins. So are situations and sums. Put two things together – jokes, images – and you get a triple harlequin. Come on! Play! Invent the world! Invent reality!' " (7). The book is a "futuristic" combination of different elements; it is a unique world, where the author is free to manipulate words, languages, time, places, events, human relationships, masks, identities, and find common elements in the most disparate aspects of the world. However, the illusion that

---

90 Boyd's (1990, 641) comment on the final part of the novel is noteworthy: "Just before Vadim rediscovers his identity he gropes about for his name, reaching comically close (Naborcroft? Nabarro?) to Nabokov. A joke, certainly, but more than that: Nabokov suggests that at this point Vadim has approached much nearer to his creator than ever before, just as Nabokov himself at the end of *Speak, Memory*, with *his* "you," remembering the birth of his own consciousness and watching over the growth of his son's, feels as near to the creative principle behind his life as he does in the creation of his art." As regards the specular elements in Nabokov's works, see Faye 2019, Ch. VI.

everything can be changed and tailored to human needs falls apart, and the writer cannot but recognize that his *nóstos* will never come true and that his world is fictitious.

7. Implicit bilingualism in Berberova's autobiographical short stories

I have discussed the major themes in Berberova's autobiography and underlined, in the introduction, the concept of implicit bilingualism that chraracterizes her works. While *The Italics Are Mine* underlines, as seen, the main socio-cultural problems that exiles deal with, Berberova voices her issues, in her short stories, by means of émigré characters, her *alter egos*, whose rootless existence is characterized by displacement and isolation. However, the Russian-American writer's stories are particular not only for the presence of foreign characters living in an alien context, facing the problems connected with cultural identity, dispossession and linguistic barriers, but also for the use of an implicit bilingualism. Despite living and writing in different contexts, Berberova actually "[...] kept the faith with her mother tongue" (Fraser 1996, 19), and never relinquished it. Since she uses none of the languages spoken in her "host countries," like English, French or German, one might wonder what makes Berberova's writings so meaningful.

To this end, I will consider two of the most symbolic short stories from the collection *The Tattered Cloak* (1990) as autobiographical writings that depict the writer's transcultural and bilingual experience. Berberova's stories embody such concepts as nostalgia, with its different overtones, and the "no man's land." Like other short stories, they are written completely in the author's mother tongue. The English readership can read Berberova only through the English translation of her works, whose characters are mostly Russian intellectuals travelling from their native country to the USA, after spending some time in some outstanding European cities[91]. Unlike Nabokov's self-translations, characterized by a lively dialogism among the languages he uses, Russian, English and French, Berberova adopts a different perspective. She avoids combining various linguistic codes and foreignisms. Her translated works read like monolingual narrative spaces, where Russian émigrés interact with the Western society of their time. Apart from the protagonists' names, Russian words and phrases are hardly ever used, and this would raise some doubts about the bilingual nature of Berberova's writings. The

---

91 The works analyzed here are English translations of Berberova's original texts written in Russian. Such translations were not done by the author, but by the translators indicated in the bibliography.

depiction of a monolingual context, however, does not prevent her texts from having a bilingual setting. Bilingualism in her prose is constantly implicit in the choice of foreign characters and specific themes. The Russian-American writer's bilingualism emerges as the stories progress, in that she addresses the English-speaking readers by presenting bilingual and transcultural issues. Although Berberova could speak English fluently, owing to her academic career in the United States, she does not explicitly unfold her bilingualism in her stories, but expresses it in an abstract and conceptual way.

One of the short stories that best illustrates such an "abstract" bilingualism is "The Black Spot," the story of the Russian immigrant Evgeny Petrovich who lives in Paris and is desperately trying to earn some money to move to the USA. To this end, he plans to redeem a pair of earrings from a pawnshop and sell them. A black spot on one of the stones in the earrings makes them worthless, yet he manages to sell them. However, he still needs more money to buy the boat ticket: "Even if I were to sell everything, leaving just the clothes on my back, my razor, and my toothbrush – it wouldn't be enough" (Berberova 1990, 221)[92]. Evgeny can finally purchase the ticket thanks to the money he receives from Alya Ivanova: "On Wednesday morning she gave me the money, and I paid for my ticket" (229). Alya is a kind of subletter who turns up at his place and asks him if she can share and pay for the room he has rented in Paris until his departure for New York; in this way she can succeed him as a renter and make sure, in accordance with the laws of the time, she has a place to stay. One of the first aspects of implicit bilingualism is represented by the hardships of the protagonist in a foreign context; Evgeny, who retraces Berberova's itinerary from Russia to the USA "via" Paris, means to change his life because he thinks that Paris does not meet his needs: the French capital, despite offering better living conditions than Saint Petersburg, is still not economically suitable. The character "[...] assumes an expulsion or absence from one's [his] native country against one's [his] will" (Kalb 2001, 141).

Exiles are often isolated and struggle to improve their living condition. As a consequence, they need to devise new contrivances to survive and to get over the barriers of communication and integration. Evgeny perceives the problems he might have to face if he chooses to live in Paris, and decides to go overseas. He continuously changes his life, and the transition from one place to another forges his self which preserves the past, but is willing to welcome, at the same time, the changes and the novelties of an unknown future. Similarly, Berberova can "[...] encompass and move beyond her external situation to integrate past and present, weaknesses and strengths, into a fully-formed self" (Kalb 2001, 142). The pro-

---

92 All subsequent quotations from *The Tattered Cloak* will refer to this edition; page numbers are given parenthetically in the text.

tagonist of the story, like the writer, means to join the different cultural spaces that he crosses.

Once arrived in New York, Evgeny meets his employer's daughter, Ludmila. His journey does not stop there and he plans to leave for Chicago. He spends hours talking with Ludmila and they travel on board a ferry without reaching the destination. The long conversations with the Russian girl takes him to an unknown dimension. The idea of not knowing their destination seems charming to them:

> Three ferries were docked, ready to sail, and we boarded one of them and immediately were struck by the carefree feeling you have when you're sailing without knowing where or when you'll be back: a rare feeling, to which you can almost never afford to succumb (260).

Evgeny has long chats with Ludmila and, owing to the aimless wandering on the ferry, he loses his time dimension:

> We had talked for twenty minutes about heaven and hell and an hour and a half about Chicago. Even if one counted another half hour for her story about her grandfather, that still didn't add up to four hours. Where had time gone? "Where has the time gone?" I exclaimed. "Where?" (251).

This sense of loss, nostalgia and uprooting torments the two immigrants. Linguistic isolation is their reaction to the problems connected with the cultural barriers. The image of the ferry lends itself to the various interpretations of nostalgia, another aspect that critics have pointed out (Lolli 2012/2013, 12-19) in Berberova's works. The two characters' choice to spend their time together on board a ferry, which can be compared to a private space of emigration, is an example of restorative nostalgia, their wish to reconstruct, to restore the lost abode; it expresses the exiles' fear to lose their original world (Mirabelli 2012, 7-8). Berberova recalls her past by means of her characters, but she does not let adverse circumstances overwhelm her, since she is steadily willing to explore new places and make the most of her rootless existence. Despite Ludmila's proposal, Evgeny decides to leave for Chicago. The past influences the exiles' life, but the writer joins it to the present in her autobiography. As Fraser (1996, 46) argues, "Her [Berberova's] whole life has been a process of conserving and of letting go – of saving the tiniest scraps for the archive while refusing to regret the passing of anything at all." Moreover, in an interview she claims that "Many things are lost. But new things will come. The new generation has no tears to shed about the end of something. They have new things to think about" (*Ibid.*). Berberova reveals her bilingualism by joining together three different space-time dimensions: the past (Russia), the present (Europe) and the future (America). She avoids writing in English and "relies" on the translations of her texts to let the English-speaking readers know them; she conveys her bilingualism through her characters' transcultural experiences. The author expresses her bilingualism by adapting to the different places she goes through and by preserving the coexistence of parallel linguistic and cultural worlds. Another example of Berberova's adaptation to different environments is at the end of the story, when Evgeny arrives in Chicago. The first impression he gains of the city is bleak:

> There was no one there, no one in the whole house, in the whole world. I went down the empty stairs, walked down the empty street to the bus. And now once again I was in a wasteland: my room was empty, the street was completely empty, and this city was empty as well (273).

Evgeny's impressions change and he can soon adapt to the new surroundings:

> "[…] I'll live again and see whether something comes of all this, after all. Even the dead are resurrected so why shouldn't I, as I'm alive?" Only for that I had to do something, I had to make a decision, get moving, adapt, I had to invent cities, people, different stories, my own life, fit in, walk in step, try to resemble other people. And it had to happen quickly, otherwise I'd turn into a vegetable (274).

The character abandons the stifling Parisian atmosphere, where his condition could not improve much, and settles into the American context. Describing this endless journey, the author means to find the only home for her, freedom. Through Evgeny she sketches a character who "carries" with him all the facets of his Russianness. At the same time, he can do without the Russian microcosm that his compatriots create. Evgeny moves to different places to improve his living condition. By joining the past and the present through her character, Berberova maps out her route, which stands for "[…] the continuation of life and culture, the creation of life and self" (Kalb 2001, 145). The American cities can be identified, therefore, with the protagonist's "no man's land," i.e. a space that is far from his motherland and from his host country. The writer expresses through Evgeny her sense of dislocation and dispossession. She finds her freedom in the imaginary dimension of her "no man's land," her private space on which nobody is allowed to trespass. As such, this space is an a-temporal abstraction, since it is not generated by a historical moment, neither is it tied to outer circumstances or real places. It has no boundaries, and is the imaginary dimension where the protagonist of the story can reveal his personality (Lolli 2012/2013, 106–127). The "no man's land" is connected with the nostalgia of the diasporic intimacy, a concept that encompasses both the past and the present. It relieves the immigrant's condition and makes him feel at his ease even overseas. It is strictly connected with the sense of intimacy experienced in the past by the immigrant in his native country and is then "extended" to the host country.

Among the other stories included in the collection *The Tattered Cloak*, "In Memory of Schliemann" is worth analyzing as well. It apparently lacks a plot and describes a bus journey along a supposedly American route: from Schliemann

Square to Great Fountains. Compared with the other stories, set mostly in Paris, "In Memory of Schliemann," like "The Black Spot," has a dynamic structure and unfolds along the never-ending itinerary of the protagonist, whose name is not given (but it can be assumed it is a man), and who visits different places. He does not mention any toponyms, apart from the names of the square, where he takes the bus, and of the destination:

> The bus sped straight down the road. Hours passed. Outside the opened window passed houses, people, cars, signs, shops. [...] I thought the sun had set, but a few minutes later it glimmered again, on the other side of the road, though not for long, it's true. The lights were already on. Dusk fell slowly. Occasionally we made a stop; people got off, others got on. A small square flashed by with a large low gray bush in the middle around which children were running, the railway passed by us, and overhead – the highway, where cars rushed headlong toward us in an unbroken chain, directly over the trains below, reminding me in a way of my dreams of life in the future (282).

The descriptions conjure up bleak places in an unnamed arid area of the USA. The weather is sultry and the places are not pleasant. The character sets out on the bus journey to take advantage of a three-day holiday from work and means to reach the coast. Although the writer does not travel across different countries, but within the borders of the USA, the protagonist sees various facets of the same area. The protagonist is disappointed by the places he visits; when he arrives at Great Fountains, what he sees is but

> [...] a square. Streetlamps burned all around. The wide, utterly bare place was surrounded by an even ring of small trees, beyond which rose buildings, tall, stone, with lights on in most of the windows. [...] Directly in front of me there was a huge, dry, cement fountain pool, about sixty meters in diameter. It was filled with people. [...] I had the impression that I was still in the middle of a large city, that in fact I hadn't gone anywhere. The purple and azure signs beyond the trees burned like the windows in the buildings (285–286).

The traveller does not like the place where he was supposed to relax. In spite of the crowd, he feels alone and soon starts thinking about a different destination. Great Fountains contradicts the charm of its name and turns out to be an alienating place. It does not meet his need for diasporic intimacy. After asking for information, he gets on another bus which takes him to a further unknown space. Once again, the journey is long: "We rolled through it now without stopping, and it seemed there would be no end to it" (289). The destination he gets to falls short of his expectations again, since the lake he means to see is polluted and a signpost marks "No swimming." The air is polluted by car exhaust and he decides to go somewhere else. He catches a train to the Gulf whose name is not given: "What Gulf?" "On the Gulf, on the sea. At the shore" (296). The sense of dislocation is increased by such continuous changes. Although the protagonist does not cross any boundaries, he voices the author's need to discover her aforementioned "no man's land," that secret corner located in her inner world where she can enjoy freedom. Berberova seems to distinguish the wasteland, which Evgeny had found in Chicago, from the "no man's land." The former is represented by the aridity and isolation of Great Fountains and of the lake, where the presence of people does not encourage the traveller to remain; the latter is an imaginary dimension that allows him to enjoy his freedom and to feel at home in an unfamiliar place. When the character arrives at the Gulf, he finally seems to find what he was looking for and can spend some time on the shore. When he returns home, he tells his supposed fiancé about his journey and explains to her who Schliemann was: he found Troy, after excavating nine cities: [...] they were lying on top of each other" (308). This explanation seems to pinpoint another aspect of exile, which was so important to Berberova's life: metaphorical exile, generated by "[...] the thoughtful complexity of artistic creation" (Kalb 2001, 141). The excavation, in fact, stands for a backward journey into the exile's memory. It is a journey across different cultural and linguistic worlds in order to find the diasporic intimacy, that familiarity with the new places that Evgeny himself was looking for during his physical exile in "The Black Spot." The long excavation that led Schliemann to discover Troy, the symbol of history and art, is the image of the protagonist's metaphorical exile, his journey of self-discovery.

The discovery of the diasporic intimacy brings to light another aspect of nostalgia. Unlike Evgeny, who expresses his restorative nostalgia to "recompose" his self and start new itineraries, the traveller of "In Memory of Schliemann" goes back in time as the journey progresses. His thoughts come to light, as well as his growing concern with the inexorable flow of time and his desire to settle in the "promised land," thus generating his reflective nostalgia. The traveller does not mean to re-create his home, but cherishes his hopes by means of his ever-increasing melancholy. The narrator focuses on his individual dimension by travelling and amplifying the distance from his home. Restorative nostalgia is shared with other exiles, while reflective nostalgia is felt by the exile who travels on his or on her own. Berberova's bilingualism emerges through the different aspects of exile and nostalgia, conveying the multiple linguistic facets of the places she crosses. Exile and nostalgia stand for the conceptual dimension of her bilingualism and her state of in-betweenness (through the characters and the situations she depicts), that is an area lying between her native country and the host country, her past and present. In spite of her in-betweenness, she maintains her double linguistic identity and decides to preserve her source language in her works. Although the characters in the two stories do not speak different languages, their state of physical and cultural hybridism is conveyed by the semantic overtones of their dialogues. The narrator's journey from Schliemann Square to the Gulf, going through Great Fountains and the lake, with the metaphorical background of the discovery of Troy, as well as Evgeny's migration from Europe to New York and then to Chicago, make the stories multi-perspective descriptions of reality. The characters' conversations and thoughts mirror the author's inner world. The conversations and the long descriptions in the two stories thus reveal a double perspective: the characters' view of the world and the writer's voice (Bakhtin 1979, 133). If, according to Bakhtin, all literary texts contain an implicit pluridiscursivity, a constant dialogue, a "negotiation" between the author and their characters, this is particularly true in Berberova's texts. Her stories reflect her plurilingual and pluridiscursive experience and bring to life, at the same time, the difficult task of tracing out the border separating fiction from the autobiographical elements[93].

8. Shteyngart's practice of bilingualism

Among the Russian writers, especially Russian-Jewish, who left their country and settled in the United States, Shteyngart anticipates modern translingual writing, though the groundwork had already been laid out, as seen, by other Russian predecessors, like Nabokov and Brodsky. Shteyngart's autobiographical book, *Little Failure*, has often been analyzed from a multicultural perspective (Bryla 2014, 89–90; Wanner 2008, 662–663), because it is about the author's life from his childhood in Russia until he moved to the USA. It illustrates, therefore, the author's education in the American multicultural setting, where he becomes a "doubly hyphenated American" (Bryla 2014, 90). The text, written in English, Shteyngart's adopted language, abounds in linguistic interferences from the Jewish and Russian worlds, and deserves particular attention from a contrastive point of view, in order to understand the extent to which translingualism and transculturalism are intertwined. Like previous translingual autobiographies, the work presents, as seen, flashbacks and flashforwards and sometimes fictionalizes the author's life, by re-writing his literary self in another language (Cooper 2018, 41). In this section I mean to carry out a brief comparative analysis of the foreign phrases used in the text, in order to single out the semantic roles of the different languages as transcultural "conveyors," and to penetrate the hybrid "fabric" of the text.

Shteyngart's nickname, "Little Failure," is emblematic, in that its sound reproduces a hybrid version of the title. It is, in fact, adapted to the Russian context by his mother as "Failurčka" (4), standing for "Little Failure," since his parents

---

93 As regards autobiographies and autobiographical works, de Man (1979, 921) says that the border between fiction and autobiography is often "imperceptible," in that autobiography is "[…] a figure of reading or of understanding that occurs, to some degree, in all texts."

used it to express their disagreement with his studies (they wanted him to be a lawyer, not a writer). "Failurčka" becomes the lexical emblem of the story. It is repeated in the text to combine two different and distant linguistic worlds through the phonetic hybridism of the word itself. It emphasizes the author's displacement in a foreign country. Shteyngart's first feelings of alienation are actually referred to his Russian childhood when, recalling a moment in Leningrad's subway, he expresses a metalinguistic comment on the words that he sees on the wall: "Those words whose power seems not only persuasive but, to a kid about to become obsessed with science fiction, they are indeed extraterrestrial. The wise aliens have landed and WE ARE THEM. And this is the language we use. The great and mighty Russian tongue" (55). The particular features of the Cyrillic characters, with the "squared" forms of the capital letters, convey a sense of estrangement in the protagonist's inner world, who does not feel part of the society he lives in and seeks "refuge" in story writing. "The great and mighty Russian tongue" (55) is thus associated with the propaganda of the Regime and affects the protagonist's solipsistic dimension. Shteyngart's choice to portray a plurilingual setting in his work is due to his early doubts about his cultural identity. He even imagines his Jewish-American *alter ego*, namely the "other" Gary that would have been born if his grandmother had married her former suitor in America. If this had happened, the hypothetical "other" Gary would have been Jewish-American, and not Jewish-Russian-American (Wanner 2012, 157–160): "Perhaps alternate-Gary would come up to me and say, 'I'm Russian, too!' And I would say, '*Ah, vy govorite po-russki?*' [*Ah, do you speak Russian?*] And he would [...] explain to me that, no, he doesn't speak Russian" (69).

I have already mentioned that Shteyngart had numerous identities and that he can be regarded as a three-time hyphenated emigrant: Jewish-Russian-American. I have also argued that Shteyngart's Jewish identity was the result of his parents' allegiance to their origins, but his Russianness had always overshadowed his Jewishness until his emigration to the USA. The writer traces back the overlapping identities to his grandparents and to their problems with their target language. As he writes: "I always thought that both of my grandmothers struggled against the despised Hebrew accent, the *Ghhhh* sound in place of the strong Russian *RRRRRR*, but when I bring it up with my father, he says empathically: 'Your grandmother *never* had a Jewish accent'" (35). As to his own experience, he says: "[...] whenever I try to flaunt my hard-perfected English, whenever my new language comes pouring out of me, I think of her [his grandmother]" (35), while his parents "[...] came to this country [the USA] stuffed with advanced degrees and keen to master the universal language of English" (35). The writer makes use of the onomatopoeic expressions to show the main phonic features of his family's languages. The "Ghhhh" sound, standing for the Jewish world, is soon replaced by the harshness of the "RRRRRR" sound, "voicing" the Russian world; the latter is, in turn, replaced by the English-American language, which the Shteyngarts are keen to learn. The sentences quoted above illustrate the linguistic passage of the writer's family from Hebrew to English through Russian. In this "linguistic map," Russian stands for the language in-between, the language that, rather than joining two linguistic worlds, marks the irreversible transition from the Jewish world to the American world.

Unlike Nabokov, who never stopped using his first language, although his emigration to the West, as I have often repeated, was a one-way itinerary, Shteyngart has been back to his birthplace, but has relinquished his source language. The numerous comparative expressions which mark the interlingual dialogue between Russian and English are frequent in the text; the writer quotes and translates into English the expression that his grandparents used to address to his father: "*Oni menja ljubili kak čërty,*" [...] *They loved me like devils*" (37). Russian belongs to the past, is the language that the writer leaves behind and uses in the text in order to "catch" a glimpse of his past. Moreover, he remembers a day, in America, when his father took him to the bus station because he did not want to spend the holidays with his family. His father kissed him goodbye and said: "*Bud' zdorov, synok,* [...] *Be well, little son*" (184). He translates some Hebrew lyrics as well, like "*Yamin, smol, smol, yamin,* left right, right, left, *trooloo-loo-loo*" (301). And when his parents are about to divorce, he quotes his answer to his mother, who claims she does not want to talk to him: "'*Nu, chorošo. Kak vam lučše.*'" Well, that's fine. Do as you please" (320). Shteyngart marks the passage that translation entails and, like Nabokov, makes the reader aware of the process of translation. In this regard, he remembers a day in which he went fishing with his father and his American friend, Jonathan, and quotes his father's Russian phrase: " '*Prochod dlja oslov!*' Papa proudly declares. 'Gary, translate.' 'It's the passage for donkeys,' I say to Jonathan" (194). His father's request to translate emphasizes Shteyngart's increasing bilingual identity. To his family, he is the linguistic "border," the interpreter of the American world. Some conversations among the characters in the text even have metalinguistic overtones, since the writer does not simply quote Russian or Hebrew words, but writes his father's English dialogues, employing particular phonic effects to underscore his foreignness. With reference to the same day, when he went fishing, he reproduces his father's Russian accent:

> "Over *zer* is mostly *flyook* and *zer* is *flaunder*...Guys, don't pull *feesh* so fast! Give him time to get on hook, okay?" [...] It occurs to me that if we had spoken English instead of Russian at home, my father would have lost some of the natural cruelty that comes with our mother tongue. *Eh, you, Snotty. Eh, you, weakling.* Because all I want to do now is to speak to Papa and Mama in Jonathan's English. Which also happens to be my own (194).

The onomatopoeic reproduction of his father's English words conveys the harshness of the Russian sounds, and the writer himself dislikes the Russian interference in his father's conversations with the local people. He underlines the difference between his English and his parents' as well, and considers himself as good as a native speaker. Shteyngart includes the "hybrid" words that his father utters and marks them in italics. They disclose the immigrant's transition to a new linguistic dimension, which the immigrant himself, Shteyngart's father, is unwilling to undergo. The presence in the passage and, in general, in the whole text, of idiomatic and slang words, like "snotty" and "weakling," stands for the writer's wish to prove that his linguistic transition has come to an end, that he can master the target language by employing its lexical and metalinguistic overtones. The use of such "hybrid" words, in fact, shows that the writer means to investigate the various registers of the language and to illustrate the phases and the problems that every immigrant has to face to settle into a different linguistic context. Some immigrants, like the writer's parents, will never overcome their linguistic barriers, owing to their adult age, which hinders their linguistic adaptation, whereas the young Shteyngart changes his attitude to the new language. His sense of isolation fades out in the text and his claimed proficiency in American English predominates.

In these examples, Shteyngart does not neglect to translate the Russian phrases and, in fact, by translating the foreign sentences into English, he aims to draw the reader's attention and to make sure that he or she understands without "getting lost" in the plurilingual text. The communication with the reader cannot cease. The writer's constant self-translation of the foreignisms into English responds to the need to maintain the phatic function, to mention one of Jakobson's linguistic functions. The phatic expression, as is known, does not exclusively imply thorough and accurate communication, since its main purpose is to avoid the loss of basic communication between the addresser and the addressee. According to Jakobson (1960, 355), the phatic function, which he ascribes to the anthropologist Malinowski, "[...] may be displayed by a profuse exchange of ritualized formulas, by entire dialogues with the mere purport of prolonging communication[94]." The message uttered by the addresser, in this case, contains short and simple sentences or phrases, like "hello," "can you hear me?" whose aim is to make sure that the speaker does not lose contact with the person he or she is talking to. By translating the Russian and Hebrew words, Shteyngart, like his predecessor Nabokov, intends to draw the reader's attention. Such foreign-

---

94 In his essay, Jakobson (1960, 355) claims that "There are messages primarily serving to establish, to prolong, or to discontinue communication, to check whether the channel works ("Hello, do you hear me?"), to attract the attention of the interlocutor or to confirm his continued attention [...]."

isms are elements of discontinuity, linguistic interferences, which the author harmoniously introduces into the text and adapts to the narrative functionality of the English macrotext.

When I analyzed Berberova's autobiography, I focused on the title and pointed out that the word *Italics* expresses the truthfulness of facts. The events are directly uttered by the narrator and reflect the setting of the autobiography. The whole title, *The Italics Are Mine*, metaphorically conveys the realism of the text. Berberova does not use italics in her autobiography, but the word *Italics* in the title conceptually affects the whole text and makes it an authentic account of her life. Shteyngart, Nabokov and, to a lesser extent, Cournos (who uses fewer foreignisms, as noted), often employ italics throughout their texts to emphasize particular words and to mark the presence of foreignisms. In particular, Cournos uses italics to highlight the few Russian and Hebrew words in the text and the numerous intertextual quotations from other English works; Nabokov's italics mark the frequent Russian and French expressions; Shteyngart writes in italics some dialogues and descriptions in English, Hebrew and Russian. The words written in italics are uttered by the writer and mark the frontiers separating the languages used in the text. Shteyngart carries out a contrastive analysis between English and Russian by means of the italic type. He increases the foreignizing effect of the text by using other characters as well, such as the block capitals, in particular when he quotes particular messages, road signs and billboards. Referring to a walk with his father, he writes:

> We are passing the five skyscraper-high, insect-like air traffic antennas down the street from us with their fearsome signage: WARNING THIS FACILITY IS USED IN FAA TRAFFIC CONTROL. LOSS OF HUMAN LIFE MAY RESULT FROM SERVICE INTERRUPTION. ANY PERSON WHO INTERFERES WITH AIRTRAFFIC CONTROL... WILL BE PROSECUTED UNDER FEDERAL LAW (201–202).

The block capitals lead the reader to a metalinguistic dimension and symbolize the immigrant's displacement. The road sign conveys coldness, detachment, depersonalization and loss of identity through the squared characters of the capital letters. Like the Cyrillic characters that he used to see in the Leningrad subway before moving to the USA, the block capitals unveil another aspect of the language, since it is used for formal communication and does not convey the emotional essence of the language as the everyday register does. The coldness of the linguistic register increases when the writer quotes messages and sentences from the screen of the computer games he plays. The graphic style changes once again and the characters of the language convey further alienation and displacement. As the lapidary messages of the road signs become more compressed within the "borders" of the screen, they reduce the emotional interaction between the speaker and the language itself. Each sentence stands isolated in its line with the symbols that are keyed in via the keyboard:

> page 120
> Embankment (Leningrad)
> P.S. This message will self-destruct in thirty hours.
> \> Drop recorder
> You wanna leave the recorder behind?
> \> Yes
> Ya shure?
> \> Yes
> Absoludly?
> \> Yes
> Todally?
> \> Yes
> I can't hear ya!
> \> Yes [...] (199)

The message contains very informal words and expresses the transience of communication. The words written on the screen will disappear, and there is no guarantee that the message will last, owing to the abstract character of software devices. The "telegraphic" communication includes slang vocabulary and very short sentences, which the author utilizes to reproduce the typical American sounds. The "technological" language, produced by means of new devices, "shortens" communication, making it essential, temporary and unemotional. Every sentence of the message is "shrunk" by the borders of the line. The lapidary communication expressed by the technological devices reflects the spirit of the American society, where life is faster and affected by the new technological era. It accentuates the writer's isolation and his attempt to interact with the new environment. Shteyngart's communication with the screen, however, fades out as well, as he shows in the following passage:

> In the dim light of Jonathan's computer room his two five-and-one-quarter-inch Apple disk drives are twirling with anticipation. The > represents the so-called status line, upon which the player would give directions. For example:
>
> \> W
>
> would mean the player wanted to go west. Or
>
> \> Open mailbox (196).

Communication is reduced to symbols and single letters. This language, which is created by the advent of technology, accounts for the choice of the themes of the stories that he writes in his early American years. His works are metafictional texts; they are stories within the writer's autobiography and disclose his inner meditations as an exile. They are set on imaginary planets and his choosing extraterrestrial places signifies his feeling of estrangement in the American society.

During his emigration to the USA, Shteyngart stops in Western Europe. When he lands in East Berlin, he hears another language for the first time, and that is his [...] first understanding that the world is not powered entirely by the great and mighty Russian tongue" (81). The writer's long stay in Western Europe, as in Nabokov's journey, led to the formation of a "third linguistic space," that is to say a "neutral" dimension where the immigrant is exposed for the first time to different languages, before the final migrating step. This third stage exerts a remarkable influence over the writer's private semiotic dimension (Lotman 1985, 58). The culture shock and the introduction of new linguistic elements into his semiosphere create new linguistic elements that he compares with his source culture. Thus, the English macrotext is interspersed, in the "European" section, with Italian and German lexis, like "Mille lire!", "Grazie mille!", "Medicina per il cuore!" (89), "über alles!", "Jungen" (84), and the autobiography exposes Shteyngart's plurilingual world. He carries out his first translation experiments in the plurilingual text, in which the combination of different signs generates an explosion of new senses (again in Lotmanian terms), as well as specular linguistic spaces.

The complex process of linguistic interference is emphasized in America, where Shteyngart realizes that "[...] the Russian language is my friend" (105), owing to his linguistic isolation and his poor knowledge of English. His mother-tongue, which he believed to be the emblem of the Soviet Regime, is now his only means of communication. The Russian language stands for the writer's identity, since it is located at the core of his semiospheric dimension (Lotman 1985, 64). On the other hand, the interaction with new linguistic elements is more dynamic along the edge of his semiospheric structure, but cannot easily modify his main linguistic structure. "English," the author writes, "is the language of commerce and work, but Russian is the language of the soul, whatever that is" (137). By interacting with new cultural contexts, the author starts his route to hybridism and self-translation, in order to carry out a more in-depth analysis of the languages that he speaks. The account of his stay in the USA is imbued with Russian and Hebrew phrases, such as "*Tot kto ne byot, tot ne lyubit.* [...] He who doesn't hit, doesn't love" (125), "'*Luchshe ne zhit'!* It is better not to live!" (126) or "*Sheket bevakasha!* 'Please be quiet'" (112), which are regularly self-translated. Shteyngart fosters a dialogue among different languages and investigates both the pluridiscursive aspect of his lexical "mosaic" and the deepest cultural layers of the foreign phrases. In Bakhtinian terms, he establishes phono-semantic and pluridiscursive connections within the wide scope of his foreignness (Bakhtin

1979, 140–141). When he recalls the conversations with his Russian-American friends in New York, he writes: "The Russian nouns lacing the barrage of English verbs, or vice versa (*"Babushka, oni poshli* shopping *vmeste v ellenvilli"* – "Grandma, they went shopping together in Ellenville," 170). He uses an English word, "shopping," in a Russian sentence to emphasize the sibilant sounds, which are frequent in Russian and have different pronunciations. As Shteyngart improves his adopted language, he writes his first story in English, whose Slavic title, "Svida," takes the reader back to his origins. Later on, he writes the "Gnorah," which, as the title suggests, centers on Jewish issues and "[…] marks the end of Russian as my primary tongue and the beginning of my true assimilation into American English" (161).

The writer's two main languages clash and interact; English overshadows his mother tongue, with the possible consequence of language attrition. Unlike his parents, whose accent, as I have previously explained, is still very strong and utter expressions like "*Ver* is man toilet?" (192), Gary claims "[…] my accent has faded and my English is strong and I can converse at a kilometre a minute" (193). Such a linguistic "contrast" explains, according to Espino Barrera (2017, 188), the immigrants' common concern, i. e. the loss of their mother-language, which often leads translingual writers to use phrases of the source language and of the target language, in order to preserve their "previous" language, their first language, in the wide universe of their linguistic in-betweenness.

As a consequence of the effects of the telegraphic communication of signs and technological devices in the modern era, we should consider Shteyngart's approach to translation from the perspective of reflexivity too. When the writer translates single "fragments," he never conceals, like Nabokov, the source "texts" and shows the "passage" of the message from the source language to the target language. Nabokov, as I have explained, often dwells on the phonic and semantic effects of the words and verses that he translates. However, the Jewish-Russian writer, naturalized American, conveys his "detachment" when he translates the foreign expressions that he uses. He tends to be less "involved" in the act of translation, since he provides the reader with the translation of the "fragments" without making his metalinguistic comments. When he writes about the ten million dollar cheque that his family thought they had won, he says: "'Mama, Papa, we won! We won! *My millionery!* We are millionaires! '*Uspokoisya*,' my father says. *Calm down*" (131). Here and in other numerous plurilingual passages, he literally translates the Russian units into English, without lingering on the choice of translation which Nabokov, instead, explains, so that the reader is familiar with his process of translation. The reflexive aspect of his translation is less "informative," because the "fragments" of the source language are not discussed or "shared" with the reader in the process of translation. In addition to his "detached" attitude to the self-translation of the foreign phrases in the text, the writer often associates some English words and letters with other possible meanings. The acronym of the Jewish school he attends, the Solomon Schechter School of Queens, is "SSSQ." He dwells on the evocations of the letters contained in the acronym: "The *S*'s are as drunk as Step-grandfather Ilya, and they're falling all over one another; the *Q* is an *O* stabbed between the legs at an angle. Often I forget the *Q* entirely, leaving just the quasi-fascistic SSS" (111). The abbreviated name of the Jewish school brings to mind the horrors of the Nazi Regime in the writer's imagination. The "deconstructing" analysis of the target language goes on as Shteyngart focuses on a particular word he often hears at the Jewish school:

> *Please work on your penmanship*, every teacher will dutifully write. *Pen* I know because it is my main toy. *Man* is someone like my father, strong enough to lift a used American air conditioner he has just bought for one hundred dollars. *Ship* is like the cruiser *Aurora* docked in Leningrad, the one that fired the fateful shot that started the October Revolution. But *pen-man-ship?* (111)

This is one of the few passages in which Shteyngart deconstructs, in the wake of Nabokov's "method," the word he means to study. Following this hermeneutic route, the writer "splits" the word into three "mono-units" and associates each unit with an object. The associations are made by employing the connotative means of the target language and carrying out an "intralingual" analysis.

Like other translingual writers of Russian origins, such as Berberova and Cournos, Shteyngart returned to Russia in 2011. His journey into the past "tests" his bilingualism or, better, the loss of his childhood language. As a matter of fact, he claims: "Granted, with my ever-growing American accent, I do not sound entirely native when I *govoryu po-russki* [speak Russian] with cabdrivers, hotel clerks, or even my good Petersburg friends" (326). Shteyngart is aware of his henolingual stage, that is the condition of linguistic *in-betweenness*, and his return to the now called Saint Petersburg increases his sense of non-belonging in a land whose language used to be his own "friend" in the American context (Espino Barrera 2017, 193). Shteyngart's familiarity with the target language is so rooted that he examines the American advertisements from a metalinguistic angle: "When I shut my eyes I hear [...] the commercial for Juicy Fruit gum sung with such intense abandon it makes me scared (*"Jew-she froooot is gonna moooove ya / it gotta taaaaste that cut raaaaght throoo ya-ugh"*) (157). The writer decomposes the single words and even "drawls" the vowel sounds in order to dwell on each word and study its own phonic peculiarities. He unveils the vowel effects employed in the American advertising to make the message more "appealing" and, from certain aspects, simpler, so that the succession of the same vowels allows any person to remember the slogan. While Berberova did not give up her source language, Cournos, Nabokov and Shteyngart had to adapt to their linguistic environments and, somehow, reverse the relationship between their source and target languages. Nabokov never relinquished his source language, as he used it to self-translate his American works, Cournos emigrated at an early age, although he spoke Russian with his family in the USA, but never used it as a literary language. Shteyngart's experience was more similar to Cournos's, in that he had to abandon his source language as a child and experienced language attrition. What differentiates the two Jewish-Russian-American writers, however, is the different mastery of their target language. For both writers, English became their mother tongue, but Cournos's linguistic evolution resulted in a simple syntactical use of the adopted language, which was suitable for foreign readers, who were unfamiliar with the most typical expressions of the target language. Apart from the local English and American jargons that he hears around and quotes in his autobiography, Cournos's narrative corpus lacks the slang and the everyday expressions of his lands of emigration, whereas *Little Failure*, being written many years later, when technology reached its peak and affected communication, presents a more informal language. The writer utilizes many slang and even vulgar expressions, combined with the new linguistic changes brought about by technology and cybernetics.

At the very end of the book, when he recalls his visit to his grandfather's grave, Shteyngart writes some words of his prayers in Hebrew and Russian, like "*Yitgaddal veyitqaddash shmeh rabba*" (349) and, for the first time, he even employs the Hebrew and Russian characters. The very last sentences of the autobiography "sum up" the plurilingual essence of the text. Shteyngart writes two Hebrew words in their original characters, transliterates them as "*Ve'imru, Amen*" (349), then translates them into English as "Let us say, Amen" (349), and into Russian as "I Skazhem: Amen!" (my transliteration, 349), using the Cyrillic letters. Shteyngart's self-translation connects the target language, English, with the languages of his DNA, Hebrew and Russian, whose characters may or may not appear in the generations to come (Apter 2006, 235). Hebrew and Russian characters are used as a consequence of a long process of plurilingual interaction; the clash of different linguistic "genes" re-awakens the recessive (non-dominant) linguistic elements. The latter, therefore, by penetrating the fragile boundaries that separate the author's languages, disclose Shteyngart's original linguistic traits and confirm his transnational identity. As Maior (2015, 125) claims about Shteyngart's identity, "[…] it is impossible to think of self as something constant: instead, it is a kind of fluid and dynamic entity that is always in motion, in a relative flux, owing to the factors that actually shape it." The end of the autobiography is Shteyngart's final and most complete example of self-translation. *Speak, Memory* and *Little Failure* partly retrace similar cultural and linguistic routes. *Little Failure* ends in the author's homeland; as such, it cannot but stand for a modern version of Nabokov's work, or its "transadaptation," to use a more "sophisticated" definition, thus reopening new "translingual negotiations" from a more modern perspective (Bryla 2014, 93)[95].

---

95 According to Stavans (2018, 27), "transadaptation" is "[…] the effort to freely re-create an established narrative in a new context. […] Of course this is an ancient practice, repackaged for our derivative, self-referential, merchandise-driven times. […] Something similar might be said of Shakespeare. Some among his thirty-seven solo plays might be described as transadaptations of a sort. *King Lear* is based on an ancient folk tale, of which a number of versions are available, including *The True Chronicle History of King Leir and His Three Daughters.*"

Conclusion

The analysis of the sociological and cultural aspects in the first part of this work aimed to define the origins of the plurilingual background of the four Russian-American writers. The research originated from the study of Nabokov's famous plurilingual *oeuvre*, as the source of much emigrant translingual literature, and extended to less known translingual intellectuals who wrote the first bilingual and plurilingual autobiographies. The investigation into such texts has focused on their plurilingual structure, representing a mosaic of foreign "verbal vestiges" (Shvabrin 2019, 340). Before the publication of Nabokov's novels, in particular *Lolita*, plurilingual writing was not common, and those Eastern European writers, like Conrad and Brodsky, who stopped using their source language as a result of their emigration, adopted their target language, without including the "remains" of their source languages in their English texts. The historical and geographical contexts support the pluridiscursive and plurilingual research as the two main coordinates that border the writers' linguistic evolution. The contrastive-pluridiscursive analysis is preceded, therefore, by the configuration of the writers' geographical spaces, in order to pinpoint the extent to which the horizontal dimensions intersect, in their autobiographies, with the diachronic depth of the historical coordinates. In contrast to Cournos, Berberova and Shteyngart, Nabokov never returned to his country and his missed temporary *nóstos* must have affected his works with the remarkable presence of plurilingual elements.

The journeys along the Euro-American route raised many problems in the writers' experiences. Every emigration from one place to another generates a strong sense of displacement, which pervades the four autobiographies. Displacement and lack of integration are linked to the law of the geographical space. The latter involves the intellectual's emigration to a new context, whose spaces, habits and culture do not suit him or her and influence his or her background. Likewise, the four writers endured great hardship, owing to the problems they faced during their emigration. The issues related to integration and displacement raise the question of everyday communication and the need to speak a different language, besides the source language. Plurilingual writing is also the expression, therefore, of the estranging effect created by the exile's sense of displacement.

As regards the linguistic aspects of the works analyzed, Cournos's autobiography shows a limited presence of foreignisms, but its narrative lay-out oozes with his bilingual and trilingual background, when Hebrew and Russian words appear in the text and are translated into the target language. Having left his country at an early age, he had to struggle with English and adopt it, because he could not employ the syntactical tools of his source language. He wrote his works in English with the purpose of hiding his imperfect knowledge of Russian and Hebrew, which, however, are sometimes used in *Autobiography*. Berberova left Russia as an adult and returned there a few years before her death, but did not switch to English in her writings. Nabokov avails himself of puns, self-translation, sound effects and strange word combinations in the plurilingual setting of his work, and this approach to writing became his peculiarity, since it was the expression of his missed return to Russia. Shteyngart, like Cournos, left his motherland early, but his work, like *Speak, Memory*, abounds in foreignisms, even though Nabokov's linguistic experiments are more sophisticated and insightful. Nabokov's incomplete journey "propelled" his linguistic experiments in his autobiography, where they are even applied to verse-writing and meter, in order to counterbalance the loss of his source language. Hence, *Speak, Memory* and *Little Failure*, as plurilingual texts in which the writers recreate their solipsistic universe, allow them to test their bilingual and trilingual skills. The particular linguistic experiments in Nabokov's two autobiographies attest to his increased nostalgia as a consequence of the effects of an eternal sense of displacement.

The combination of the space-time dimensions, the former standing for the synchronic level of the narration, the latter standing for its diachronic level, underlies the structure of the autobiographies. The synchronic perspective, which is mostly descriptive, is associated with the space-time relationships among different geographical areas, with the present time of the narration, the time related to the account of the geographical route, which is illustrated in the cartographic organization of the text. The diachronic perspective evokes the writers' deepest childhood memories. They emerge as linguistic "fragments" originated from the memory of specific past moments in which the writers used to speak their mother tongue. The diachronic level constitutes, therefore, the linguistic axis of the texts, namely their linguistic evolution; it recalls, in the present time of the synchronic space, the memories associated with the source language. The coexistence of the two perspectives stands out in *Autobiography*, in which the synchronic level overshadows the diachronic level, since the text mainly describes the writer's itinerary and evokes the geographical places he went through. In particular, Cournos's work revolves around its "earthly" setting, in that it often has the structure of a travel document, even though it does not lack the writer's reflections on his past. This narrative structure that, at times, recalls Defoe's style in *Robinson Crusoe* (1719), provides the reader with detailed information about the place and the time of his journeys: it is a document that retraces the writer's route and its toponymic labyrinth.

Speak, Memory presents a different space-time configuration, since it mainly brings to light Nabokov's reflections on his childhood, his thoughts and the linguistic influence that his Russian and foreign tutors had on him. The space references are less frequent and the linguistic "fragments" originating from the evocation of the past appear in the text, often creating the pretext for making "bizarre" contrastive analyses among the languages that are involved. The diachronic dimension, therefore, stands out in *Speak, Memory*, by "filling" the few space references with numerous discourses on time, languages, life and the past. The work is a valuable document that explains Nabokov's different linguistic stages and the development of his plurilingual identity. The description of Nabokov's identity continues in *Look at the Harlequins!*, which extends his journey to the USA and then back to Russia. The narration of Nabokov's imagined return to Russia, his imagined *nóstos*, expresses his frustration at not being able to see his country again. The author reconstructs his imaginary visit to Russia by considering the stories he heard and read about other emigrants' return to the motherland.

Berberova deserves a special place in this analysis, since she does not relinquish her source language in her writings. Although her autobiography and stories are written entirely in Russian and then translated into English, she expresses a different form of bilingualism. The title of her work, *The Italics Are Mine*, foreshadows that all the events and facts narrated in it are not masked or distorted, as occurs in Nabokov's novels, whose characters are often unreliable because of their multiple identities. Berberova's autobiography reveals the facts as they are, as if they were uttered by her and written in italics. The main concepts in her writings are linked to nostalgia and its different aspects. Berberova expresses her reflective nostalgia, since she describes her life among the émigrés she met in Europe and in the USA and retraces her cultural and linguistic evolution. She expresses, at the same time, her restorative nostalgia, in that she tends to reconstruct her original context by meeting the Russian *literati* abroad. Her life among the Russian émigrés takes place within the borders of a recreated space of emigration, a "no man's land," namely a place inhabited by her compatriots only, and where her national culture has different characteristics.

The concept of nostalgia has been applied to Nabokov as well, but with a different overtone. His overt connection with the past attests to his will to recall the days mostly spent with his tutors. More than evoking his past and, therefore, expressing his restorative nostalgia, Nabokov remembers his efforts to settle in new environments, thus recreating the nostalgia of the diasporic intimacy. The latter aims to make the writer feel at ease in the foreign context, so that he can communicate with an apparently alienating context. Nabokov's two autobiographies, the real one and the fictional one, join together different linguistic "fragments," owing to the eternal dialogue between the writer and his foreign environment. Such "fragments" allow him to interact with the foreign context and recreate a plurilingual environment, where interlingual communication is not hindered by language barriers.

Shetyngart follows Nabokov's experience and sets it in a more modern perspective. The plurilingual autobiographies create a semiospheric space, where the dialogue between different linguistic codes occurs along the edge of the semiospheric circle itself. Different languages introduce and impose new words and expressions, mixing linguistic elements of source and target languages. In particular, Nabokov and Shteyngart recreate their plurilingualism through the sudden introduction of foreign elements into their linguistic world. The combination of such elements results, at times, in strange plurilingual and plurisemantic words and phrases, which make the two writers' worlds linguistically dynamic. The combination of the linguistic and cultural "fragments" leads to the linguistic explosion, using Lotman's term, with the generation of new senses and meanings. Berberova's text, in contrast to *Speak, Memory* and *Little Failure*, does not deal with such linguistic experiments, in that her work is written in Russian and became famous among the English-speaking people in its English translation. The osmotic exchange that occurs in Nabokov's and Shteyngart's works is much more limited in *The Italics Are Mine* and in her stories, whose bilingualism implicitly comes to light throught the description of the Russian emigrants' life in Europe and in the USA, and in the evocation of their motherland. Cournos can be regarded as one of the "fathers" of modern linguistic and cultural emigration from Russia to the USA through Europe. His autobiographical account does not present Nabokov's and Shteyngart's linguistic discourses, neither does it express implicit bilingualism, as discussed for Berberova. Words and expressions connected with Cournos's motherland sometimes appear. Such expressions are not merged with the target language, but are introduced into the text and pave the way for a "basic" interaction with the author's target culture.

Owing to the intertextual and interlingual dialogism that Cournos, Nabokov, Berberova and Shteyngart foster with literary works and voices from other cultural worlds, the bakhtinian pluridiscursivity is a useful perspective for analysis to "unearth" some of the most relevant transcultural elements in the writers' works. The plurilingual approach of these works brings back the "palimpsests" of previous writings. Despite using different linguistic codes, they conjure up the cultural background of their writers' homeland and transpose it to a new setting. The pluridiscursivity of these plurilingual autobiographies is characterized, therefore, by their constant evocation of previous works and voices from the past. Nabokov, in particular, who "leads" this research, since he is the father of plurilingual experimentalism, discloses his Russian hypotext in *Speak, Memory* when he investigates his linguistic and biographical "minutiae." In these pages I have often used the prefix "pluri" to refer to the concepts of abundance, variety and diversity. This prefix, actually, is well-associated with the idea that lies behind any emigrant's experiences. Emigrating means going through different peoples and cultures. Emigrating multiplies identities, languages, the uncertainties that the exile has to face. The emigrant lives in a fluid dimension, where every element is subject to sudden changes, negotiations, discussions. Thus, the emigrant writers try to narrate their experiences in their plurilingual writings, since the combination of different languages in their texts blurs the linguistic boundaries and every word turns out to be unreliable, changeable, deceitful and plurisemantic.

The constant interlingual relationship among different worlds in the autobiographies highlights the writer's attempt to involve the readers in the process of linguistic integration; it aims to make the readers feel at ease with a plurilingual context they are not used to. The translation of the foreign "fragments" into the target language expresses the linguistic function that Jakobson called phatic, because the translation of the *impromptu* foreignisms means to draw the reader's attention to the process of translation. Such self-translation gradually "removes" the linguistic frontiers that mark the texts. The frontiers, which are still visible in Cournos and Berberova, become blurred in Nabokov and Shteyngart, whose metalinguistic discourses endow them with particular powers. Accordingly, they have the privilege of looking at their texts from different linguistic perspectives and from both sides of their blurred frontiers. Nabokov and Shteyngart can look at their plurilingual world both from the marginal perspectives of their texts, where the frontiers lie, to dwell on the linguistic passage from one side of the border to the other, and from the central angle of the text, characterized by its homolinguistic structure, where the writer can linger on the peculiarities of a specific language.

Bibliography

Affuso, Olimpia. 2012. "Nostalgia: un atteggiamento ambivalente." *Sociologia italiana – AIS Journal of Sociology* 1: 105–24.
Antonucci, Alessia. 2004. "*Il corsivo è mio:* viaggio attraverso la memoria di Nina Berberova." *eSamizdat* II: 41–50.
Appel, Alfred. 1967. "An Interview with Vladimir Nabokov." *Wisconsin Studies in Contemporary Literature* 8, no. 2 (Spring): 127–52.
–. 1967. "An Interview with Vladimir Nabokov." In *Nabokov. The Man and his Work*, edited by L. S. Dembo, 19–44. Madison, Milwaukee and London: The University of Wisconsin Press.
Apter, Emily. 2006. *The Translation Zone: a New Comparative Literature*. Princeton: Princeton University Press.
Ayers, David. 2011. "John Cournos and the Politics of Russian Literature in *The Criterion*." *Modernism* 18, no. 2 (April): 355–69.
Baetens Beardsmore, Hugo. 2008. "Multilingualism, Cognition and Creativity." *International CLIL Research Journal* 1 (1): 4–19.
Bakhtin, Mikhail. 1975. *Vaprosy literatury i estetiki*. Moskva: Izdatelstvo Khudozhestvennaya Literatura (It. transl.: 1979. *Estetica e romanzo*, edited by Clara Strada Janovic. Torino: Einaudi).
Barker, Murl G. 1994. "In Memoriam. Nina Nikolaevna Berberova 1901–1993." *The Slavic and East European Journal* 38, no. 3 (Autumn): 553–56.
Barthes, Roland. 1953. *Le degré zéro de l'écriture*. Paris: Éditions du Seuil (It. transl.: 2003. *Il grado zero della scrittura. Seguito da Nuovi saggi critici*, edited and translated by Giuseppe Bartolucci, Renzo Guidieri, Leonella Prato Caruso, Rosetta Loy Provera. Torino: Einaudi).
Basch, Linda, Cristina Blanc-Szanton, and Nina Glick Schiller. 1992. "Transnationalism: a New Analytic Framework for Understanding Migration." *Annals of the New York Academy of Sciences* 645, no. 1 (July): 1–24.
Bauer, Patricia J., Leif Stennes, and Jennifer C. Haight. 2003. "Representation of the inner self in autobiography: Women's and men's use of internal states language in personal narratives." *Memory* 11 (1): 27–42.
Bellini, Paola Mirina. 2000. *Scrivere di sè*. Flavia Ravazzoli (pref.). Pavia: Ibis.
Berberova, Nina. 1990. *The Tattered Cloak*, edited and translated by Marian Schwartz. New York: New Directions Classics.

–. 1972. *Kursiv moj: avtobiografiia.* München: W. Fink Verlag (En. transl.: 1993. *The Italics Are Mine*, translated by Philippe Radley. New York: Vintage Books).
Bontila, Ruxanda. 1999. "Shifting Relations in Nabokov's *Speak, Memory*." *British and American Studies* 4 (1): 67–72.
Boyd, Brian. 1990. *Vladimir Nabokov. The Russian Years*. Princeton: Princeton UP.
–. 1991. *Vladimir Nabokov. The American Years*. Princeton: Princeton UP.
–. 2011. *Stalking Nabokov. Selected Essays*. New York: Columbia University Press.
Boyd, Brian, and Tolstoy Anastasia, eds. 2019. *Vladimir Nabokov. Think, Write, Speak. Uncollected Essays, Reviews, Interviews and Letters to the Editor*. London: Penguin Classics.
Boym, Svetlana. 2011. "Nostalgia." *Atlas of Transformation*. http://monumenttotransformation.org/atlas-of-transformation/html/n/nostalgia/nostalgia-svetlana-boym.html (accessed June 10, 2019).
Bozovic, Marijeta. 2018. "Nabokov's Translations and Transnational Canon Formation." *Translation Studies* 11 (2): 172–84.
Brauner, David. 2017. "The Sons of Phil: Rothian Self-Satire and Self-Incrimination in Shalom Auslander's *Foreskin's Lament* and Gary Shteyngart's *Little Failure*." *Open Library of Humanities* 3 (2): 1–26. Doi: https://doi.org/10.16995/olh.143.
Brodsky, Joseph. 1995. *On Grief and Reasons. Essays*. New York: Farrar, Straus and Giroux.
–. 1996. "La mia vita è un'astronave," edited by Gabriella Caramore. *Micromega* 3: 153–66.
Bryla, Martyna. 2018. "Tracking the Transnational Trickster: Gary Shteyngart and his Protagonists." *Nordic Journal of English Studies* 17 (2):1–28.
–. 2018. "Narrating oneself, narrating America: Gary Shteyngart's *Little Failure* (2014)." In *Broadening Horizons. A Peak Panorama of English Studies in Spain*, edited by María Beatriz Hernández Pérez, Manuel Brito Marrero, and José Tomás Monterrey Rodríguez, 89–96. San Cristóbal de La Laguna: Servicio de Publicaciones de la Universidad de La Laguna.
Carosso, Andrea. 1999. *Invito alla lettura di Nabokov*. Milano: Mursia.
Cesereanu, Ruxandra. 2006. "*Homo Viator* in Transition Travelling through and with Céline, Nabokov, Kerouak." *Cahiers de l'Echinox* 11: 34–9.
Cojocaru, Alina. 2017. "Spatialized time, synchrony and the art of memory in Vladimir Nabokov's *Speak, Memory*." *Bulletin of the Transilvania University of Braşov. Series IV: Philology and Cultural Studies* 10 (1): 109–16.
Connolly, Julian W. 2005. "Chronology." In *The Cambridge Companion to Nabokov*, edited by Julian W. Connolly, xv–xxiii. New York: Cambridge University Press.
Cooper, Sara-Louise. 2016. "Contesting the Unconscious: Frederic W. Myers and Vladimir Nabokov's *Speak, Memory: An Autobiography Revisited*." *Journal of Modern Literature* 39 (4): 19–32.
–. 2018. "Translating Timelessness: The Relationship between Vladimir Nabokov's *Conclusive Evidence, Drugie berega*, and *Speak, Memory: An Autobiography Revisited*." *The Modern Language Review* 113, no. 1 (January): 39–56.
Cornwell, Neil. 2005. "From Sirin to Nabokov: the Transition to English." In *The Cambridge Companion to Nabokov*, edited by Julian W. Connolly, 151–69. New York: Cambridge University Press.
Cournos, John. 1935. *Autobiography*. New York: G. P. Putnam's Sons.

–. 1960. "An Environment for Writers." *New York: Saturday Review Associates* 43, no. 1 (October): 13–5.

Coye Heard, Frederick. 2016. "Time Travelers. Narrative Space-Time and the Logic of Return in Nabokov's American Fiction." *Texas Studies in Literature and Language* 58, no. 2 (Summer): 144–64.

Cronin Michael. 2000. *Across the Lines: Travel, Language, Translation*. Cork: Cork University Press.

Dadashova, Shafag. 2016. "Auto-translation and Nabokov's autobiography." *TradTerm* 28: 76–88.

de la Durantaye, Leland. 2014. "The Purpose of Autobiography, or the Fate of Vladimir Nabokov's *Speak, Memory*." In *The Cambridge Companion to Autobiography*, edited by M. Di Battista, and E. O. Wittman, 165–79. Cambridge: Cambridge UP.

de la Puente, Ines García. 2015. "Bilingual Nabokov: Memories and Memoirs in Self-Translation." *Slavic and East European Journal* 59 (4): 585–608.

de Man, Paul. 1979. "Autobiography as De-facement." *MLN Comparative Literature* 94, no. 5 (December): 919–30.

Delage-Toriel, Lara. 2017. "Speak, Mademoiselle. Nabokov's Authorial Posture Revisited." In *Nabokov's Women. The Silent Sisterhood of Textual Nomads*, edited by Elena Rakhimova-Sommers, 209–26. Lanham, Boulder, New York, London: Lexington Books.

Dembo, L. S. 1967. "Selected Bibliography of Nabokov's Works." In *Nabokov. The Man and his Work*, edited by L. S. Dembo, 277–78. Madison, Milwaukee and London: The University of Wisconsin Press.

Diment, Galya. 2005. "Nabokov's biographical impulse: art of writing lives." In *The Cambridge Companion to Nabokov*, edited by Julian W. Connolly, 170–84. Cambridge: Cambridge University Press.

Edwards, John. 2013. "Bilingualism and Multilingualism: Some Central Concepts." In *The Handbook of Bilingualism and Multilingualism*, edited by Tej K. Bathia, and William C. Ritchie, 5–25. Oxford: Wiley-Blackwell.

Espino Barrera, Tomás. 2017. "Salvaging the Mother Tongue in Exile." *Comparative Critical Studies* 14 (2–3): 187–204.

Farwell, Erik. 2018. "'There Are Incredible Reservoirs of Anger Sloshing Around Our Country': An Interview with Gary Shteyngart." *Hazlitt*, September 4, 2018. https://hazlitt.net/feature/there-are-incredible-reservoirs-anger-sloshing-around-our-country-interview-gary-shteyngart (accessed September 1, 2019).

Faye, Sabine. 2019. *Nabokov. Le jeu baroque*. Paris: CNRS Éditions.

Finkelstein, Miriam. 2016. "Re-Writing Tolstoevskii: Postcolonial Narratives in Contemporary Russian-American Literature." In *Postcolonial Slavic Literatures after Communism*, edited by Klavdia Smola, and Dirk Uffelmann, 453–77. Frankfurt am Main: Peter Lang.

Foucault, Michel. 1984. "Des espaces autres. Hétérotopies." *Architecture, Mouvement, Continuité* 5: 46–9 [En. transl.: 1986. "Of Other Spaces," translated by Jay Miskowiec. *Diacritics* 16, no. 1 (Spring): 22–7].

Fraser, Kennedy. 1996. *Ornament and Silence. Essays on Women's Lives from Edith Wharton to Germaine Greer*. New York: Vintage Books.

Friedman, Natalie. 2004. "Nostalgia, Nationhood, and the New Immigrant Narrative: Gary Shteyngart's The Russian Debutante's Handbook and the Post-Soviet Experience." *Iowa Journal of Cultural Studies* 5 (1): 77–87.

Gan, Gregory. 2019. "'And With Me, My Russia/I Bring Along in a Travelling Bag': Literary and Ethnographic Narratives of Russian Exile and Emigration, Past and Present." *Revolutionary Russia* 32, no. 1 (May): 154–79.

Genette, Gérard. 1972. *Figures III*. Paris: Éditions du Seuil (It. transl.: 1976. *Figure III. Discorso del Racconto*, translated by Lina Zecchi. Torino: Einaudi.

Giorcelli, Cristina. 2008. "Prefazione." In *Lo sguardo esiliato. Cultura europea e cultura Americana fra delocalizzazione e radicamento*, edited by Cristina Giorcelli and Camilla Cattarulla, 9–14. Napoli: Casoria.

Godayol, Pilar. 2000. *Espais de frontera. Génere i Traducció*. Barcelona: Eumo Editorial (It. transl.: 2002. *Spazi di frontiera. Genere e traduzione*, edited and translated by Annarita Taronna. Bari: Palomar.

Gold, Herbert. 2003. "Interview with Vladimir Nabokov." In *Vladimir Nabokov's Lolita. A Casebook*, edited by Ellen Piffer, 195–206. Oxford: Oxford University Press.

Gómez, Maria Asunción Barreras. 2015. "The Divided Self Metaphor: a Cognitive-Linguistic Study of two Poems by Nabokov." *International Journal of English Studies* 15 (1): 97–113.

Grayson, Jane. 2001. *Vladimir Nabokov*. Woodstock & New York: Overlook Press.

Grinberg, Marat. 2014. "The Hollowing of Gary Shteyngart. On leaving (and not quite leaving) Russia." *Commentary* 138, no. 1 (July-August): 69–71.

Grosjean, François. 2019. *A Journey in Languages and Cultures. The Life of a Bicultural Bilingual*. Oxford: Oxford UP.

Grundy, John G., and Kalinka Timmer. 2017. "Bilingualism and working memory capacity: A comprehensive meta-analysis." *Second Language Research* 33 (3): 325–40.

Hamrit, Jacqueline. 2019. *Frontières et limites dans l'oeuvre de Vladimir Nabokov*. Mauritius: Éditions universitaires européennes.

Hetényi, Zsuzsa. 2018. "Translating Self-Translation and the Units of the Translation: the Case of Nabokov." *Studia Slavica Academiae Scientiarum Hungaricae* 63 (1): 49–55.

Hoffman, Dominique. 2011. *Without Nostalgia. Nina Berberova's Short Fiction of the 1930s*. Dissertation. https://doi.org/10.17615/smqw-z602 (accessed September 11, 2019).

Jakobson, Roman. 1960. "Closing statement: Linguistics and Poetics." In *Style in Language*, edited by Thomas A. Sebeok, 350–77. New York, London: The Technology Press of Massachusetts Institute of Technology and John Wiley & Sons, Inc.

–. 1959. "On Linguistic Aspects of Translation." In *On Translation*, edited by Reubern Arthur Browen, 232–39. Cambridge (MA): Harvard University Press.

Kadiu, Silvia. 2019. *Reflexive Translation Studies. Translation as Critical Reflection*. London: UCL Press.

Kalb, Judith E. 2001. "Nina Berberova: Creating an Exiled Self." *Russian Literature* 50, no. 2 (August): 141–62.

Klein, Melanie. 1963. *Our Adult World and Other Essays*. New York: Basic Books (It. transl.: 1984. *Il nostro mondo adulto e altri saggi*. Firenze: Martinelli).

Kroll, Judith F. 2017. "The bilingual lexicon. A window into language dynamics and cognition." In *Bilingualism. A framework for understanding the mental lexicon*, edited by

Maya Libben, Mira Goral, and Gary Libben, 27-48. Amsterdam, Philadelphia: John Benjamins Publishing Company.
Kuek, Florence, and Ling, Tek Soon. 2017. "Autobiography and Ethical Literary Criticism." *Interlitteraria* 22 (2): 282-96.
Laufer, Batia, and Baladzhaeva, Liubov. 2015. "First language attrition without second language acquisition. An exploratory study." *International Journal of Applied Linguistics* 166, no. 2 (January): 229-53.
Livak, Leonid. 2007. "L'émigration russe et les élites culturelles françaises 1920-1925. Les débuts d'une collaboration." *Cahiers du Monde russe* 48, no. 1 (January-March): 23-44.
Lolli, Francesca. 2012/2013. *Nostalgia, identità, no man's land nella prosa di Nina Berberova. Oltre il ritratto della Russia emigrata*. Dissertation. http://dspace.unive.it/bitstream/handle/10579/3880/826190-74506.pdf?sequence=2 (accessed August 11, 2019).
Lotman, Yurij M., and Uspenskij, Boris A. 1975. *Tipologia della cultura*, edited by Remo Faccani, Marzio Marzaduri, translated by Manila Barbato Faccani, Remo Faccani, Marzio Marzaduri, Sergio Molinari. Milano: Bompiani.
Lotman, Yurij M. 2000. *Semiosfera. Kul'tura i vzryv. Vnutri myslyaschikh mirov. Stat'i. Issledovaniya. Zametki*. Sankt-Peterburg: Isskustvo-SPB (It. transl.: 1985. *La semiosfera. L'asimmetria e il dialogo nelle strutture pensanti*, translated by Simonetta Salvestroni. Venezia: Marsilio).
–. 1993. *Kul'tura i vzryv*. Moskva: Gnosis (It. transl.: 1993. *La cultura e l'esplosione. Prevedibilità e imprevedibilità*, translated by Caterina Valentino. Milano: Feltrinelli).
Lyaskovets, Tetyana. 2014. "Time, Photography, and Optical Technology in Nabokov's *Speak, Memory*." *CLCWeb: Comparative Literature and Culture* 16, no. 3 (September): 1-9.
Magarotto, Luigi. 2007. "Per una tipologia dell'emigrazione russa." *Europa Orientalis* 26: 127-44.
Maior, Enikő. 2015. "The Question of Identity in Gary Shteyngart's *Little Failure*." *Acta Universitatis Sapientiae, Philologica* 7 (1): 123-32.
Maklakova, Natalia Vasilevna, Khovanskaya, Ekaterina Sergeevna, and Grigorieva, Leona L. 2017. "An Investigation into Self-Translation." *Journal of History Culture and Art Research* 6, no. 4 (September): 1260-67.
Marrone, Gianfranco. 2018. *Prima lezione di semiotica*. Bari-Roma: Laterza.
Meade, Gabriela, and Dijkstra, Ton. 2017. "Mechanisms underlying word learning in second language acquisition." In *Bilingualism. A framework for understanding the mental lexicon*, edited by Maya Libben, Mira Goral, and Gary Libben, 49-72. Amsterdam, Philadelphia: John Benjamins Publishing Company.
Mirabelli, Chiara. 2012. "Nostalgie. Sguardi sul dolore del ritorno." https://www.scuolaphilo.it/download/Mirabelli-Nostalgie-Philo-2012.pdf: 1-8 (accessed May 10, 2019).
Moro, Andrea. 2018. *I confini di Babele. Il cervello e il mistero delle lingue impossibili*. Bologna: Il Mulino (En. transl.: 2008. *The Boundaries of Babel. The Brain and the Enigma of Impossible Languages*, translated by Ivano Caponigro, and Daniel B. Kane. Cambridge, London: The MIT Press).
Nabokov, Vladimir Vladimirovich. 1941. "The Art of Translation." https://newrepublic.com/article/62610/the-art-translation (accessed August 27, 2019).
–. 1966. *Speak, Memory: An Autobiography Revisited*. New York: Capricorn Books.

–. 1975. *Eugene Onegin. A Novel in Verse. Volume I. Introduction and Translation*, translated by Vladimir Nabokov. Princeton: Princeton University Press.
–. 1973. *Strong Opinions*. New York: McGraw-Hill (Second ed. 1990. *Strong Opinions*. New York: Vintage Books).
–. 2016. *Letters to Vera*, edited and translated by Olga Voronina, and Brian Boyd. London: Penguin Classics.
–. 1974. *Look at the Harlequins!*. New York: McGraw-Hill (Third ed. 2017. *Look at the Harlequins!* London: Penguin Classics. It. transl.: 2012. *Guarda gli arlecchini!*, translated by Franca Pece. Milano: Adelphi).
Nafisi, Azar. 2019. *That Other World. Nabokov and the Puzzle of Exile*, edited by Azar Nafisi and Valerie Miles, translated from Persian by Lotfali Khonij. New Haven & London: Yale University Press.
Nöth, Winfried. 2006. "Yuri Lotman on metaphors and culture as self-referential semiospheres." *Semiotica* 161 (1/4): 249–63.
Pavlenko, Aneta. 2009. "Conceptual Representation in the Bilingual Lexicon and Second Language Vocabulary Learning." In *The Bilingual Mental Lexicon. Interdisciplinary Approaches*, edited by Aneta Pavlenko, 125–60. Bristol, Buffalo, Toronto: Multilingual Matters.
Peterson, Nadya L. 2001. "The Private 'I' in the Works of Nina Berberova." *Slavic Review* 60, no. 3 (Autumn):491–512.
Pitzer, Andrea. 2013. *The Secret History of Vladimir Nabokov*. New York, London: Pegasus Books.
Ponomareff, Constantin V. 2013. "The Metaphor of Loss in V. Nabokov's *Speak, Memory*." *Queen's Quarterly* 120, no. 3 (Fall): 402–13.
Possamai, Donatella. 2018. *Al crocevia dei due millenni. Viaggio nelle letteratura russa contemporanea*. Padova: Esedra.
Roper, Robert. 2015. *Nabokov in America. On the Road to Lolita*. New York: Bloomsbury.
Rothermel, Paulina. 2014. "Vladimir Nabokov: A Case Study of Multilingualism and Translation." *Styles of Communication* 6 (1): 130–38.
Russo, Michele. 2015. *Iosif Brodskij. Saggi di letture intertestuali*. Milano: LED.
Sapir, Edward. 1921. *Language. An Introduction to the Study of Speech*. New York: Hartcourt Brace (It. transl.: 2007. *Il linguaggio. Introduzione alla linguistica*, edited by Paolo Ramat. Torino: Einaudi).
Satterthwaite, Alfred. 1976. "John Cournos and 'H. D.'" *Twentieth Century Literature* 22, no. 4 (December): 394–410.
Schmid, Monika S., and Barbara Köpke. 2017. "The relevance of first language attrition to theories of bilingual development." *Linguistic Approaches to Bilingualism* 7 (6): 637–67.
Schwartz, Lynne Sharon. 2014. "From Russia, with Anxiety." *Moment; Washington* 39, no. 2 (March-April): 72–3.
Scura, Carla. 2008. "Vladimir Nabokov o dell'indicibile libertà dell'esilio." In *Lo sguardo esiliato. Cultura europea e cultura americana fra delocalizzazione e radicamento*, edited by Cristina Giorcelli, and Camilla Cattarulla, 391–409. Napoli: Loffredo Editore.
Slavkov, Nikolay. 2015. "Language attrition and reactivation in the context of bilingual first language acquisition." *International Journal of Bilingual Education and Bilingualism* 18 (6): 715–34.
Shteyngart, Gary. 2014. *Little Failure: A Memoir*. London: Penguin Books.

Shields, David. 2009. "Autobiography as Criticism, Criticism as Autobiography." *The Iowa Review* 39, no. 1 (Spring): 150–52.

Shvabrin, Stanislav. 2019. *Between Rhyme and Reason. Vladimir Nabokov, Translation, and Dialogue.* Toronto: University of Toronto Press.

Smith, Marilyn Schwinn. 2013. "The London Making of a Modernist: John Cournos in Babel." In *American Writers in Europe. 1850 to the Present*, edited by Asya Ferdâ, 75–96. Basingstoke: Palgrave MacMillan US.

Springer, Carl Carsten. 2002. "Nabokov's Memory at Play: *Look at the Harlequins!*." *Amerikastudien* 47 (3): 359–74.

Stavans, Ilan. 2018. *On Self-Translation. Meditations on Language.* Albany: State University of New York Press.

Steiner, George. 1970. "Extraterritorial." *Triquarterly* 17: 119–27.

Swan, Melanie. 2016. "Bergson's Qualitative and Its Link to Free Will and Subjectivation." In *Spatiality and Temporality: An Interdisciplinary Approach*, edited by Ingrida Eglė Žindžiuvienė, 13–23. Warsaw: IRF Press.

Takahashi, Tomoko. 2019. "Autobiographical self-translation – translator as the author, narrator and protagonist." *The Translator*: 1–12. doi: 10.1080/13556509.2019.1588932.

Tlustý, Jan. 2012. "Fictional and Factual Autobiography from the Perspective of Speech Act Theory." *Organon F: Medzinárodný Časopis Pre Analytickú Filozofiu* 19: 179–85.

Todorov, Tzvetan. 1981. *Mikhaïl Bakhtine. Le principe dialogique suivi de Écrits du Cercle de Bakhtine.* Paris: Éditions du Seuil (It. transl.:1990. *Michail Bachtin. Il principio dialogico*, translated by Anna Maria Marietti. Torino: Einaudi).

–. 1982. *La conquête de l'Amérique. La question de l'autre.* Paris: Éditions du Seuil (It. transl.: 2014. *La conquista dell'America. Il problema dell'«altro»*, edited by Pier Luigi Crovetto, translated by Aldo Serafini. Torino: Einaudi).

Trousdale, Rachel. 2011. "Nabokov and the Transnational Canon." *The Nabokovian* 66: 7–14.

Voronina, Olga. 2017. "'They are All Too Foreign and Unfamiliar…': Nabokov's Journey to the American Reader." *Metacritic Journal for Comparative Studies and Theory* 3 (2): 25–51.

Wanner, Adrian. 2008. "Russian Hybrids: Identity in the Translingual Writings of Andreï Makine, Wladimir Kaminer, and Gary Shteyngart." *Slavic Review* 67, no. 3 (Fall): 662–81.

–. 2012. "Russian Jews as American Writers: A New Paradigm for Jewish Multiculturalism?" *Melus* 37, no. 2 (Summer): 157–76.

–. 2017. "Poems and Problems: Vladimir Nabokov's Dilemma of Poetic Self-Translation." *SEEJ* 61, no. 1 (March): 70–91.

–. 2018. "The poetics of displacement: Self-translation among contemporary Russian-American poets." *Translation Studies* 11, no. 2 (May): 122–38.

Wellek, Rene, and Austen Warren. 1956. *Theory of Literature.* New York: Harcourt, Brace & World, Inc. Wilson, Rita. 2009. "The Writer's Double: Translation, Writing, and Autobiography." *Romance Studies* 27, no. 3 (July): 186–98.

Winnicot, Donald W. 1965. *The Maturational Processes and the Facilitating Environment: Studies in the Theory of Emotional Development.* London: Karnac Books (It. transl.: 2007. *Sviluppo affettivo e ambiente. Studi sulla teoria dello sviluppo affettivo*, translated by A. Bencini Bariatti. Roma: Armando).

Worthy, Jo, Idalia Nuñez, and Katherine Espinoza. 2016. "Wow, I get to choose now!" Bilingualism and biliteracy development from childhood to young adulthood." *Bilingual Research Journal* 39, no. 1 (January): 20–34.

Wyllie, Barbara. 2016. "Shape-Shifters, Charlatans, and Frauds: Vladimir Nabokov's Confidence Men." *The Cambridge Quarterly* 45, no. 1 (March): 1–19.

Index of Names

Affuso, Olimpia   45, 127
Antonucci, Alessia   29, 127
Appel, Alfred   19, 73, 75, 127
Apter, Emily   66, 118, 127
Ayers, David   15, 71, 127

Baetens Beardsmore, Hugo   13, 127
Bakhtin, Mikhail   12, 68, 86, 102, 109, 115, 127
Baladzhaeva, Liubov   9, 131
Barker, Murl G.   27, 127
Barthes, Roland   54, 74, 127
Basch, Linda   65, 127
Bauer, Patricia J.   26, 127
Bellini, Paola Mirina   40, 127
Berberova, Nina   5, 8-9, 11, 13, 15-16, 26-33, 38, 40-41, 47-48, 50, 54-63, 74, 103-109, 113, 117, 121-125, 127, 130-132
- "In Memory of Schliemann"   106-108
- "The Black Spot"   104, 107-108
- *The Italics Are Mine*   11, 26-27, 31-32, 40-41, 54, 56, 103, 113, 123-124, 128
- *The Tattered Cloak*   103-104, 106, 127
Blanc-Szanton, Cristina   65, 127
Bontila, Ruxanda   79, 128
Boyd, Brian   19-20, 22, 30, 52, 73, 75, 81, 90-91, 102, 128, 132
Boym, Svetlana   43, 128
Bozovic, Marijeta   65, 72, 128
Brauner, David   33, 51, 128
Brodsky, Joseph   13, 28, 43, 51, 56, 62, 81, 109, 121, 128
Bryla, Martyna   33, 37, 109, 119, 128

Carosso, Andrea   9, 128
Cesereanu, Ruxandra   84, 128
Cojocaru, Alina   23, 25, 128
Connolly, Julian W.   9, 128-129
Cooper, Sara-Louise   9, 74, 76, 109, 128
Cornwell, Neil   20-21, 128
Cournos, John   5, 9, 13, 15-18, 20, 22, 26-27, 32-33, 38, 41-49, 54-58, 61-63, 65-73, 97, 113, 117-118, 121-122, 124-125, 127-128, 132-133
- *Autobiography*   15-19, 23, 26-27, 33, 42, 44, 56, 65-66, 70-72, 122, 128
- *Babel*   17, 70-71, 133
- *The Mask*   17, 71
Coye Heard, Frederick   21, 129
Cronin, Michael   70, 129

Dadashova, Shafag   22, 129
de la Durantaye, Leland   9, 65, 73, 129
de la Puente, Ines García   9, 129
de Man, Paul   39, 109, 129
Delage-Toriel, Lara   80, 129
Dembo, L. S.   9, 127, 129
Dijkstra, Ton   9, 131
Diment, Galya   82, 129

Edwards, John   7, 129
Espino Barrera, Tomás   15, 72, 116-117, 129
Espinoza, Katherine   8, 134

Farwell, Erik   62, 129
Faye, Sabine   102, 129
Finkelstein, Miriam   19, 129

Foucault, Michel   44, 129
Fraser, Kennedy   28, 31, 58, 103, 105, 129
Friedman, Natalie   37, 130

Gan, Gregory   20, 30, 130
Genette, Gérard   34, 39, 130
Giorcelli, Cristina   44, 130, 132
Glick Schiller, Nina   65, 127
Godayol, Pilar   72, 130
Gold, Herbert   80, 130
Gómez, Maria Asunción Barreras   40, 130
Grayson, Jane   9, 24, 130
Grigorieva, Leona L.   87, 131
Grinberg, Marat   59, 63, 130
Grosjean, François   18, 130
Grundy, John G.   7, 130

Haight, Jennifer C.   26, 127
Hamrit, Jacqueline   88, 130
Hetényi, Zsuzsa   8, 21, 130
Hoffman, Dominique   42, 130

Jakobson, Roman   69, 86, 112, 125, 130

Kadiu, Silvia   88, 130
Kalb, Judith   28, 32, 104, 106, 108, 130
Khovanskaya, Ekaterina Sergeevna   87, 131
Klein, Melanie   50, 130
Köpke, Barbara   8, 90, 132
Kroll, Judith F.   7, 130
Kuek, Florence   40, 90, 131

Laufer, Batia   9, 131
Ling, Tek Soon   40, 90, 131
Livak, Leonid   30, 131
Lolli, Francesca   48, 56, 105–106, 131
Lotman, Yurij M.   10, 36, 43, 56–57, 60, 90, 115, 124, 131–132
Lyaskovets, Tetyana   47, 82, 131

Magarotto, Luigi   19, 131
Maior, Enikő   33–34, 118, 131
Maklakova, Natalia Vasilevna   87, 131
Marrone, Gianfranco   10, 60, 131
Meade, Gabriela   9, 131

Mirabelli, Chiara   43, 80, 105, 131
Moro, Andrea   11, 131

Nabokov, Vladimir Vladimirovich   5, 7–9, 11–13, 15–16, 19–27, 29–32, 34, 37–38, 41, 46–54, 56–58, 61–62, 65, 71–103, 109, 111–113, 115–118, 121–125, 127–134
- *Eugene Onegin. A Novel in Verse*   94, 132
- *Letters to Vera*   132
- *Lolita*   13, 75, 84, 99, 121, 130, 132
- *Look at the Harlequins!*   5, 91–94, 97–98, 100–102, 123, 132–133
- *Speak, Memory: An Autobiography Revisited*   5, 9, 12, 21–23, 26–27, 33, 38–39, 46–49, 51, 53, 67, 73–77, 79–80, 83–84, 88–94, 98, 101–102, 118, 122–125, 128–129, 131–132
- *Strong Opinions*   92, 132
- *The Gift*   101
- *The Real Life of Sebastian Knight*   21, 101
Nafisi, Azar   9, 25–26, 91, 96, 101, 132
Nöth, Winfried   60, 132
Nuñez, Idalia   8, 134

Pavlenko, Aneta   7, 132
Peterson, Nadya L.   27, 74, 132
Pitzer, Andrea   20, 30, 132
Ponomareff, Constantin V.   9, 23, 73, 132
Possamai, Donatella   19, 132

Roper, Robert   53, 132
Rothermel, Paulina   12, 83, 132
Russo, Michele   62, 81, 132

Sapir, Edward   10, 132
Satterthwaite, Alfred   15, 132
Schmid, Monika S.   90, 132
Schwartz, Lynne Sharon   35, 132
Scura, Carla   54, 56, 82, 132
Shteyngart, Gary   5, 9, 11–13, 15–16, 32–38, 41, 48, 56, 58–63, 97–98, 109–119, 121–122, 124–125, 128–133

- *Little Failure: A Memoir* 12, 33–34, 38, 61–63, 98, 109, 118, 122, 124, 128, 131–132
Shields, David 41, 133
Shvabrin, Stanislav 94, 121, 133
Slavkov, Nikolay 9, 132
Smith, Marilyn Schwinn 69, 73, 133
Springer, Carl Carsten 91, 101, 133
Stavans, Ilan 119, 133
Steiner, George 79, 89, 133
Stennes, Leif 26, 127
Swan, Melanie 26, 82, 133

Takahashi, Tomoko 13, 133
Timmer, Kalinka 7, 130

Tlustý, Jan 39, 133
Todorov, Tzvetan 40, 45, 100, 133
Trousdale, Rachel 65, 133

Voronina, Olga 73, 89, 132–133

Wanner, Adrian 15–16, 67, 83, 90, 109–110, 133
Warren, Austen 75, 133
Wellek, Rene 75, 133
Wilson, Rita 89, 133
Winnicot, Donald 50, 133
Worthy, Jo 8, 134
Wyllie, Barbara 77, 134

Passages – Transitions – Intersections
Paola Partenza, Andrea Mariani (eds.)

Volume 6: Pier Carlo Bontempelli
Alles ist nur Symbol
20208. 128 Seiten, paperback
€ 25,– D
ISBN 978-3-8471-1001-9

Volume 5: Paola Partenza (ed.)
Sin's Multifaceted Aspects in Literary Texts
2018. 140 Seiten, paperback
€ 25,– D
ISBN 978-3-8471-0852-8

Volume 4: Alessandro Giovannucci
Perspectives historico-esthétiques dans l'œuvre de Fernando Liuzzi
2018. 118 Seiten, paperback
€ 25,– D
ISBN 978-3-8471-0841-2

Volume 3: Greta Colombani
A gordian shape of dazzling hue
Serpent Symbolism in Keats's Poetry
2017. 126 Seiten, paperback
€ 25,– D
ISBN 978-3-8471-0775-0

Volume 2: Andrea Mariani
Italian Music in Dakota
The Function of European Musical Theater in U.S. Culture
2017. 250 Seiten, paperback
€ 35,– D
ISBN 978-3-8471-0655-5

Volume 1: Paola Partenza (ed.)
Dynamics of Desacralization
Disenchanted Literary Talents
2015. 179 Seiten, paperback
€ 35,– D
ISBN 978-3-8471-0386-8

Vandenhoeck & Ruprecht Verlage

 unipress · www.vandenhoeck-ruprecht-verlage.com